SIGNAL IN THE NOISE

Mastering the Art and Science of Data-Driven Discovery

Elizabeth Onasanya

Published by **AvidBook publishing Agency**

Dedication

To the curious minds who refuse to accept that correlation equals causation, who question the obvious, and who seek truth in the wilderness of information. To the practitioners who bridge the gap between data and wisdom, transforming numbers into narratives that matter. And to the future generations of data scientists, analysts, and decision-makers who will carry forward the noble pursuit of separating signal from noise in an increasingly complex world.

Contents

Foreword

In an era when data has become the new oil, the ability to extract meaningful insights from massive amounts of data has never been more important. However, as our ability to collect and store data has increased exponentially, our collective understanding of what that data means has not kept up. Despite having unprecedented access to information, we are frequently more confused, polarized, and uncertain than ever before.

This book stems from a simple but profound realization: the future belongs not to those who can generate the most data, but to those who can find the most meaning in it. The art and science of data-driven discovery is more than just a technical discipline; it is a way of thinking, a methodology for dealing with uncertainty, and, ultimately, a pathway to better decision-making in all aspects of life.

These pages are more than just a technical manual; they also provide a philosophical framework for thinking about information, uncertainty, and discovery. The principles presented here have been tested in boardrooms and laboratories, financial markets and medical research, political campaigns, and social movements. They are the result of decades of experience helping individuals and organizations make better decisions in the face of complexity and uncertainty.

Preface

The inspiration for this book came from a frustrating realization I had during my early career as a data analyst. Despite having access to sophisticated tools, powerful computers, and massive datasets, I found myself repeatedly making poor decisions based on what appeared to be sound analysis. The issue wasn't technical ability; I could write complex queries, build statistical models, and create compelling visualizations. The problem was that I hadn't learned to think clearly about what information could and couldn't tell me.

This experience set me on a path that has taken me across multiple decades and industries, from healthcare to finance and technology startups to government agencies. Along the way, I've seen countless examples of organizations drowning in data but thirsting for insight. I've witnessed brilliant technical minds create analyses that were mathematically correct but practically useless. I've seen decision-makers ignore clear signals because they don't fit their preconceived notions, while chasing noise because it confirms their bias.

This book's methodology evolved as a result of these experiences. It draws on a variety of disciplines, including statistics, psychology, computer science, design, philosophy, and behavioral economics, because the task of extracting meaning from data is inherently multidisciplinary. Whether you're deciding on a career path, evaluating a medical treatment, or comprehending a political poll, the fundamental challenges of distinguishing signal from noise apply.

The approach taken here is deliberately pragmatic. While we will cover theoretical concepts, the emphasis will always be on application. Each chapter contains frameworks, tools, and methodologies that can be immediately applied to real-world problems. The goal is not to train you to be a statistician or a computer scientist, but to develop you into a better thinker capable of navigating uncertainty with confidence

Introduction

We live in a data-driven world, but we are often more confused than ever. Every day, we are bombarded with data, charts, trends, and predictions. Social media provides us with a steady stream of correlations and conclusions. News organizations compete to present the most compelling narrative, supported by the most recent data. Businesses make millions of dollars in decisions based on dashboard metrics that may or may not reflect reality. Politicians craft policies based on studies that may or may not be reliable.

In this environment, the ability to distinguish between meaningful patterns and random fluctuations in signal and noise has emerged as one of the most valuable 21st-century skills. However, it is a skill that is rarely taught systematically and is frequently misunderstood at its core.

The central idea behind this book is that data-driven discovery is both an art and a science. It is a science because it uses rigorous methodologies, statistical principles, and systematic approaches to data collection and analysis. It is an art because it takes intuition, creativity, and judgment to know which questions to ask, which methods to use, and how to interpret results in context.

The signal and noise metaphor is derived from communications engineering, where engineers must design systems that can reliably transmit information in the face of interference. In the context of data analysis and decision-making, the signal represents the true patterns, relationships, and insights that can assist us in understanding the world and making better decisions. The noise represents everything else, including random fluctuations, measurement errors, irrelevant correlations, and deceptive patterns that can lead us astray.

The difficulty is that in most real-world scenarios, signal and noise are inextricably linked. Unlike in engineering, where noise can often be filtered out using technical means, in data analysis, noise frequently looks identical to the signal. A correlation may indicate a genuine causal relationship, or it may be a complete coincidence. A trend may indicate a fundamental shift or a temporary fluctuation. A pattern can reveal deep insights or be an artifact of data collection or processing.

This ambiguity is not a flaw in the system; it is a necessary aspect of working with data about complex, dynamic, and uncertain phenomena. The goal is not to completely eliminate uncertainty, which is impossible, but to manage it intelligently and make decisions that are robust to various data interpretations.

Throughout the book, we will look at the tools, techniques, and mindsets that enable effective data-driven discovery. We will look at how successful analysts approach problems, design investigations, and communicate their findings. We will investigate common pitfalls and biases that can derail even the most sophisticated analyses.

1

THE DATA RENAISSANCE FROM INFORMATION OVERLOAD TO INSIGHT

Throughout most of human history, information was scarce and valuable. Knowledge was concentrated in the hands of a select few scribes, scholars, and institutions with the means to collect, preserve, and transmit information across time and space. Although the printing press democratized access to information, knowledge creation and distribution remained expensive and time-consuming. Decision-makers at all levels, from farmers planning crops to monarchs planning wars, had to make do with limited information and rely heavily on experience, intuition, and tradition.

This scarcity-based approach to information fostered mental habits that have lasted into the modern era. Information was hoarded because it was deemed valuable. Waiting for additional information was rarely an option, so decisions were made quickly. Expertise was defined more by what you knew than by your ability to learn and adapt to new situations.

The digital revolution has fundamentally changed the landscape. Today, we generate more data in a single day than in all of human history prior to the year 2000. Every click, transaction, sensor reading, and social media post contributes to an ever-increasing mountain of data. Businesses can track customer behavior in real time, governments can continuously monitor economic indicators, and researchers can access datasets that were unimaginable just a few decades ago.

This shift from scarcity to abundance has created unprecedented opportunities, but it has also brought new challenges. The issue is no longer accessing information but making sense of what we have. The bottleneck has moved from collection to comprehension, storage to synthesis, and data to wisdom.

Consider the evolution of weather forecasting as a case example. For centuries, weather prediction was based on local observations, folklore, and pattern recognition with limited data. A farmer may predict rain based on animal behavior, cloud formations, or traditional sayings passed down through generations. These methods were often surprisingly effective for local, short-term predictions, but their scope and accuracy were limited by design.

The introduction of systematic data collection weather stations, balloon launches, and satellite imagery progressively improved forecasting accuracy. However, the real breakthrough occurred when meteorologists learned to process massive amounts of data using sophisticated mathematical models. Today's weather forecasts combine information from thousands of sensors, satellite images, radar data, and supercomputer-powered computer simulations. The challenge is no longer gathering enough data but rather integrating all available data to make coherent, actionable predictions.

This same pattern, from data scarcity to data abundance to the challenge of data synthesis, has played out in almost every aspect of human activity. In the past, doctors relied heavily on direct observation and limited diagnostic tools. They now have access to lab results, imaging studies, genetic profiles, and electronic health records, but the challenge is to combine all of this data into accurate diagnoses and treatment plans.

In the past, managers made decisions based on quarterly reports and surveys. Today, they can monitor performance in real time using dashboards that show hundreds of metrics, but the challenge is determining which metrics are important and how they relate to business outcomes.

The abundance of data has also resulted in new types of noise that did not exist in the era of information scarcity. When information was expensive to collect and process, a natural filter eliminated a lot of irrelevant data. Today, when storage is inexpensive and collection is automatic, we frequently collect everything, whether it is useful or not. This creates what researchers refer to as the "curse of dimensionality," which states that as we measure more variables, the likelihood of finding spurious correlations increase exponentially.

Furthermore, the democratization of data analysis tools means that more people than ever before are creating analyses, but not all of them are properly trained. The internet is full of charts, graphs, and statistics created by well-meaning people who may not understand the limitations of their methods or how to interpret their findings correctly.

The transition from information scarcity to information abundance necessitates a fundamental shift in how we approach knowledge and decision-making. During the scarcity era, the goal was to collect as much relevant information as possible. In the abundance era, the goal is to efficiently filter, synthesize, and interpret information. This necessitates new skills, tools, and ways of thinking about the relationship between data and insight.

Successful navigation of this new landscape necessitates what we might call "information metabolism," the ability to consume, process, and derive nutrition from the massive amounts of information available to us while avoiding the negative effects of information overload. Just as physical metabolism allows us to extract energy from food while removing toxins, information metabolism allows us to extract insights from data while eliminating noise and misinformation.

This metabolic approach to information necessitates both technical proficiency and conceptual frameworks. On the technical side, we require tools for data processing, statistical analysis, and visualization that can handle large, complex datasets. On the conceptual level, we require frameworks for thinking about causation, uncertainty, and evidence that will help us avoid common pitfalls and biases.

The data renaissance is about more than just having more information; it's about learning how to use that information effectively. This wisdom includes not only technical competence but also judgment, creativity, and ethical responsibility. The practitioners who master this combination of skills will not only survive the data deluge but will use it to create unprecedented value for themselves and their organizations.

The Psychology of Pattern Recognition in Human Decision-Making

Humans are natural pattern recognition machines. This ability, developed over millions of years of evolution, enabled our ancestors to survive in complex and dangerous environments. Recognizing the rustling of leaves that might indicate a predator, determining which plants were safe to eat based on their appearance, or predicting weather patterns based on subtle environmental cues was literally a matter of life and death.

The same pattern recognition ability that served us so well in our evolutionary environment can help and hinder us in today's data-rich world. On the one hand, our intuitive ability to recognize patterns enables us to quickly identify potentially significant relationships in complex data. Experienced analysts frequently talk about having a "feel" for data, which allows them to quickly identify anomalies or interesting trends. On the other hand, our pattern recognition systems evolved in a very different environment to the one we now live in, and they can lead us astray when applied to modern datasets.

One of the most important characteristics of human pattern recognition is its high sensitivity to salient, memorable examples while being relatively insensitive to base rates and statistical regularities. The availability heuristic refers to our tendency to overestimate recent, vivid, or emotionally significant events when making predictions or judgments.

For example, after a widely publicized plane crash, many people will avoid flying, even though the statistical risk of air travel has not changed. The vivid, memorable nature of the crash makes it appear more probable than it is. Similarly, in business, managers may overreact to recent customer complaints or sales losses while undervaluing larger statistical trends that provide a more accurate picture of performance.

Another important feature of human pattern recognition is our tendency to see patterns even in random data. This tendency, known as apophenia, reflects the fact that our pattern detection systems evolved to be extremely sensitive. It was preferable to see a predator that didn't exist than to miss one that did. In data analysis, this can lead to the identification of "insights" that are actually random noise.

A classic example of this phenomenon is the "hot hand" fallacy in basketball, where players, coaches, and fans believe that a player who has made several shots in a row is more likely to make the next shot. Statistical analysis has shown that, in most cases, consecutive shots are statistically independent; the hot hand is largely an illusion created by our tendency to see patterns in random sequences.

The human tendency to impose narrative structure on data is another double-edged aspect of our pattern recognition abilities. Humans are storytelling creatures, and we naturally try to construct coherent narratives to explain the patterns we observe. This can be extremely valuable for communicating insights and making data actionable, but it can also lead us to oversimplify complex phenomena or to construct causal stories where none actually exist.

Consider the challenge of interpreting stock market movements. Financial markets generate enormous amounts of data, and there is constant pressure to explain why prices moved in a particular direction on any given day. Financial journalists and analysts are skilled at constructing plausible narratives to explain market movements, but research has shown that most short-term price movements are essentially random and that the explanations offered are usually post-hoc rationalizations rather than genuine insights into market dynamics.

Understanding these psychological tendencies is crucial for effective data analysis because it allows us to design processes and use tools that leverage our natural strengths while compensating for our weaknesses. For example, knowing that we are prone to availability bias suggests that we should systematically collect and review base rate information rather than relying on recent examples. Knowing that we tend to see patterns in random data suggests that we should use statistical significance testing and other techniques to verify that apparent patterns are not just noise.

One of the most effective strategies for managing the psychological challenges of pattern recognition is to approach data analysis as a collaborative process rather than an individual one. Different people will notice different patterns and will be subject to different biases. By bringing multiple perspectives to bear on the same dataset, we can often identify insights that would be missed by any individual analyst and avoid errors that might result from individual biases.

Another important strategy is to make the process of pattern recognition more systematic and explicit. Rather than relying purely on intuition, effective analysts develop standard procedures for exploring data, testing hypotheses, and validating conclusions. This doesn't eliminate the role of intuition; indeed, intuition often guides the most important discoveries, but it provides a framework for testing and refining intuitive insights.

The goal is not to eliminate human judgment from data analysis, which would be both impossible and undesirable, but to create systems and processes that amplify our natural pattern recognition abilities while minimizing the impact of our cognitive biases. This requires a deep understanding of both the strengths and limitations of human cognition, as well as the technical tools and methods that can support more effective decision-making.

Ultimately, the most successful data analysts are those who understand themselves as well as they understand their data. They recognize their own biases and blind spots, they know when to trust their intuition and when to demand additional evidence, and they have developed systematic approaches for transforming raw pattern recognition into reliable insights.

Building the Foundation: Essential Mindsets for Data-Driven Discovery

The transition from intuition-based decision-making to data-driven discovery necessitates more than just technical abilities; it necessitates a fundamental shift in mindset. This shift entails adopting new ways of thinking about uncertainty, evidence, and knowledge, which may appear counterintuitive or uncomfortable at first, but are required for effective analysis in complex, data-rich environments.

The first important mindset is what we might call "probabilistic thinking." Traditional decision-making frequently operates on a binary basis: something is either true or false, good or bad, likely or unlikely. Data-driven discovery necessitates thinking about probabilities and levels of confidence. Rather than asking whether a hypothesis is true, we ask how confident we can be in its validity based on available evidence. Instead of looking for definitive answers, we seek the best available estimates based on current information.

This probabilistic mindset extends to how we approach our own analyses and conclusions. Effective data analysts maintain an appropriate level of confidence that they are neither overly certain about conclusions based on limited evidence nor inappropriately uncertain about conclusions supported by multiple lines of evidence. They understand that all analyses are subject to uncertainty, but they also recognize that this uncertainty does not render the analysis worthless; rather, it requires that uncertainty be explicitly acknowledged and managed.

The second key mindset is "systems thinking." Individual data points rarely tell complete stories on their own. They derive their meaning from their context within larger systems of relationships, feedback loops, and causal mechanisms. Effective data analysts develop the ability to see individual observations as parts of larger wholes, to understand how different variables influence each other, and to recognize that changing one part of a system may have unexpected effects on other parts.

Systems thinking also involves understanding the difference between correlation and causation and recognizing that causal relationships in complex systems are often subtle, indirect, and time delayed. A marketing campaign may not show immediate effects on sales, but it may influence brand awareness, which influences customer consideration, which eventually influences purchasing behavior. Understanding these multi-step causal chains is essential for designing effective interventions and for avoiding simplistic interpretations of data.

The third essential mindset is "experimental thinking." Rather than viewing analysis as a process of finding definitive answers, experimental thinking approaches analysis as a process of testing hypotheses and learning from results. This mindset emphasizes the importance of formulating clear, testable hypotheses before beginning analysis; of designing analyses that can actually test those hypotheses; and of interpreting results in light of what they do and don't tell us about our initial questions.

Experimental thinking also involves embracing failure as a source of learning. In traditional decision-making contexts, being wrong is often seen as a failure to be avoided. In data-driven discovery, being wrong is often a necessary step toward being right. The key is to be wrong quickly and cheaply, to learn from those mistakes, and to incorporate that learning into subsequent analyses.

The fourth essential mindset is "meta-cognitive awareness" thinking about thinking. Effective data analysts develop the ability to step back from their analyses and examine their own thought processes. They ask questions like, What assumptions am I making? What biases might be influencing my interpretation? What alternative explanations haven't I considered? How confident should I be in this conclusion?

This metacognitive awareness extends to understanding the limitations of different analytical methods and tools. Every statistical technique, every visualization method, and every data source has strengths and weaknesses. Understanding these limitations is crucial for choosing appropriate methods and for interpreting results correctly.

The fifth essential mindset is "collaborative humility." Data-driven discovery is rarely a solitary activity. The most important insights often emerge from the intersection of different perspectives, different areas of expertise, and different ways of thinking about problems. This requires the ability to work effectively with others, to communicate technical concepts to non-technical audiences, and to integrate feedback from stakeholders who may not have analytical backgrounds but who have deep domain expertise.

Collaborative humility also involves recognizing that data analysts are not the only ones with valuable insights. Subject matter experts, customers, front-line employees, and other stakeholders often have intuitions and observations that can guide analysis in productive directions or highlight important factors that might not be apparent in the data alone.

The sixth essential mindset is "ethical responsibility." Data analysts wield significant influence over decisions that affect individuals, organizations, and societies. With this influence comes responsibility to use data fairly, accurately, and transparently. This involves technical responsibilities using appropriate methods, avoiding misleading presentations, and acknowledging limitations but it also involves broader ethical considerations about privacy, consent, fairness, and the potential for analyses to reinforce existing inequalities or create new forms of discrimination.

Developing these mindsets requires practice, reflection, and often a willingness to challenge deeply held beliefs about how knowledge is created and how decisions should be made. It requires moving from a world where expertise is defined by what you know to a world where expertise is defined by how well you can learn, adapt, and think clearly about complex problems.

The reward for developing these mindsets is the ability to navigate complexity with confidence, to find meaningful patterns in chaotic data, and to make decisions that are grounded in evidence while remaining appropriately humble about what that evidence can and cannot tell us. These skills are not just valuable for professional data analysts; they are increasingly essential for anyone who wants to make effective decisions in a data-rich world.

2

THE ANATOMY OF SIGNAL AND NOISE UNDERSTANDING WHAT MATTERS

In the realm of data analysis, the concept of "signal" represents the heart of what we're searching for: the meaningful patterns, relationships, and insights that can inform better decisions and deeper understanding. Yet defining what constitutes a signal is more nuanced and context-dependent than it might initially appear. Signal is not simply any pattern we can identify in data; rather, it is a pattern that provides useful information about the underlying phenomena we're trying to understand.

To grasp the true nature of signal, we must first understand that it exists only in relation to purpose. A pattern that represents a strong signal for one question might be pure noise for another. Consider a dataset of customer purchase transactions. If our goal is to understand seasonal buying patterns, then the regular fluctuations in sales volume throughout the year represent an important signal. However, if our goal is to detect credit card fraud, those same seasonal patterns might be noise that obscures the irregular patterns we're actually looking for.

This purpose-dependent nature of signal has profound implications for how we approach data analysis. It means that effective analysis must begin not with the data itself, but with clear articulation of what questions we're trying to answer and what kinds of patterns would be meaningful in that context. The same dataset can yield entirely different signals depending on the lens through which we examine it.

Signal also has a temporal dimension that is often overlooked. What constitutes meaningful information depends not only on our current questions but also on the time horizon we're considering. Short-term fluctuations that appear to be noise when viewed over a long time period might actually represent important signals about immediate phenomena. Conversely, long-term trends that are invisible in short-term data might represent the most important signals of all.

Consider the challenge of monitoring a manufacturing process. Minute-to-minute variations in product quality might appear to be random noise, but they could actually signal important changes in equipment condition, raw material quality, or environmental conditions. At the same time, gradual deterioration in average quality over months or years might be invisible in day-to-day monitoring but could represent crucial signals about systematic problems that require attention.

Another important aspect of signal is its relevance to actionability. Information that cannot be acted on, even if it represents true patterns in data, may not be a useful signal for decision-making. This is not to say that non-actionable patterns are worthless; they may provide important insights that inform our understanding of underlying mechanisms, but we must distinguish between intellectually interesting signals and signals that are practically useful.

The signal strength varies significantly across contexts and domains. In some fields, such as physics or engineering, we can often identify very strong signals with high confidence because the underlying systems obey well-known laws, and we can account for many confounding factors. In other fields, such as economics or psychology, signals are weaker and more ambiguous because the systems are more complex, confounding factors are more difficult to control, and the phenomena being studied may be inherently more variable.

Understanding the expected strength of signal in various domains is critical for establishing appropriate expectations and selecting appropriate analytical methods. Methods that work well for detecting strong signals in clean data may not be suitable for detecting weak signals in noisy data, and vice versa.

Signal has an important relationship with scale and aggregation. Patterns that appear invisible at one level of analysis may become visible at another. Individual customer behaviors may appear random and unpredictable, but when combined with thousands of customers, clear patterns may emerge. In contrast, patterns that appear in aggregate data may obscure important variations at the individual level.

This multi-scale nature of the signal is especially important in the age of big data, when we can analyze phenomena at multiple levels of granularity at the same time. The key insight is that different levels of analysis frequently reveal different types of signals, and the most complete understanding is often obtained by examining patterns across multiple scales.

Another important factor to consider is the signal's reliability and reproducibility. True signal should withstand reasonable changes in analytical methods, data sources, and time periods. Patterns that appear only when data is analyzed in a specific way, or that disappear when slightly different methods are used, are more likely to be analysis artifacts rather than genuine insights into underlying phenomena.

This emphasis on robustness has significant implications for how we carry out and validate our analyses. It implies that we should routinely test our findings with various methods, subsets of data, and analytical hypotheses. It also implies that we should be especially skeptical of findings that appear to rely heavily on specific methodological choices.

Finally, a signal must be interpreted in light of the larger context of knowledge and understanding. The most valuable signals are frequently those that confirm important theoretical predictions, challenge established assumptions or reveal previously unknown relationships. A signal that simply confirms what we already know with high confidence, while not worthless, may be less valuable than a signal that extends our understanding in new directions.

This contextual nature of signal explains why domain expertise is so crucial for effective data analysis. Understanding what would be surprising, what would be theoretically important, and what would be practically significant requires deep knowledge of the field in question. The most powerful analyses often occur at the intersection of statistical sophistication and domain expertise, where technical analytical skills are combined with deep understanding of the underlying phenomena.

The Many Faces of Noise: Systematic vs. Random Interference

While signal represents the meaningful patterns we want to find, noise includes all of the factors that interfere with our ability to detect and interpret those patterns. Understanding the various types of noise and their characteristics is critical for developing effective noise-management strategies. Noise is not a single, uniform phenomenon; it comes in a variety of forms, each requiring unique approaches to identification and mitigation.

The most fundamental distinction between noise types is random noise versus systematic noise. Random noise is made up of unpredictable fluctuations that lack an identifiable or modellable underlying pattern or cause. These fluctuations could be the result of measurement errors, inherent variability in the phenomena under study, or the influence of numerous small, unobservable factors. Random noise is distinguished by its lack of correlation with other variables and tendency to average out over large samples or time periods.

In contrast, systematic noise is made up of patterns that interfere with our ability to detect signals but are not random. These patterns could be the result of data collection biases, unaccounted-for confounding variables, or measurement or analysis artifacts. Unlike random noise, systematic noise does not average out over larger samples; in fact, it may become more noticeable as sample sizes increase.

The distinction between random and systematic noise is critical because it determines which strategies are most effective for dealing with each type. Random noise can frequently be reduced using techniques such as averaging, smoothing, or increasing sample size. However, systematic noise necessitates different approaches. We may need to change our data collection methods, account for confounding variables in our analysis, or completely redesign our analytical approach.

Measurement noise represents one of the most common forms of interference in data analysis. Every measurement process introduces some degree of error, whether from limitations in measurement instruments, variations in measurement conditions, or human error in recording or processing measurements. Understanding the characteristics of measurement noise in your specific context is essential for interpreting results correctly.

Some measurement noise is relatively benign; it introduces random variations that can be smoothed out through appropriate statistical techniques. Other measurement noise is more problematic because it introduces systematic biases. For example, if a survey instrument consistently misrepresents certain types of responses, or if a sensor systematically drifts over time, the resulting noise can seriously distort our conclusions.

Sampling noise arises from the fact that we rarely have access to complete populations; instead, we work with samples that may not accurately represent the larger populations we are attempting to understand. Random sampling noise can be quantified and managed using statistical methods, but systematic sampling biases can be far more problematic.

Consider the difficulties encountered by political pollsters. Random sampling error, or the differences that occur by chance when surveying different groups of people, can be estimated using standard statistical formulas. However, systematic sampling biases, such as the tendency of certain types of people to respond more or less frequently to polls, are much more difficult to detect and correct. These systematic biases have been responsible for some of the most visible polling failures in recent years. Temporal noise refers to variations over time that interfere with our ability to detect meaningful patterns. Some temporal noise is random, unpredictable fluctuations that occur for no apparent reason. However, much temporal noise is systematic, reflecting regular patterns such as seasonal variations, day-of-week effects, or long-term trends that may be irrelevant to the phenomenon we're attempting to understand. For example, if we want to assess the effectiveness of a new marketing campaign, we must consider seasonal variations in sales, regular promotional cycles, and long-term growth patterns. Failure to account for these temporal patterns may cause us to attribute changes in performance to our intervention when they are actually the result of these background temporal processes.

Confounding is one of the most insidious types of systematic noise because it can give the appearance of meaningful relationships where none exist, or it can conceal genuine relationships that do exist. Confounding occurs when a third variable influences both of the variables being studied, resulting in spurious correlations or concealing genuine causal relationships.

The classic example of confounding is the observed relationship between ice cream sales and drowning deaths. These two variables are positively correlated, but that does not imply that ice cream consumption causes drowning. Instead, a third variable, temperature, influences both the desire for ice cream and the likelihood of swimming activities that may result in drowning accidents. Confounding detection and control necessitates extensive domain knowledge as well as meticulous analytical design. Statistical techniques can aid in identifying potential confounders but understanding which variables may be confounders and how to account for them necessitates extensive knowledge of the field in question.

Algorithmic noise represents a growing category of interference that results from the computational processes we use to collect, store, and analyze data. Data compression algorithms might introduce artifacts, machine learning algorithms might create spurious patterns through overfitting, and data processing pipelines might introduce systematic biases through their design choices.

As our analytical processes become more complex and automated, understanding and controlling algorithmic noise becomes increasingly important. This requires not just statistical sophistication but also a deep understanding of the computational tools and processes we're using.

Environmental noise encompasses all the external factors that can influence our data but that are not directly related to the phenomena we're studying. This might include changes in economic conditions, weather patterns, regulatory changes, or cultural shifts that affect behavior in ways that interfere with our ability to detect the patterns we're interested in.

The key to managing environmental noise is often through careful experimental design that either controls these factors or randomizes their effects across different conditions. When experimental control is not possible, statistical techniques for controlling for known environmental factors become crucial. Understanding the different types of noise and their characteristics is essential for developing effective analytical strategies. The goal is not necessarily to eliminate all noise, which is often impossible, but to understand how different types of noise might affect our conclusions and to develop approaches that are robust to the types of noise we're likely to encounter. This understanding also helps us set appropriate expectations for our analyses. In some contexts, noise levels are inherently high, and we should expect our signals to be weak and our conclusions to be tentative. In other contexts, noise levels are low, and we should be able to detect strong signals with high confidence. Matching our analytical expectations to the noise characteristics of our specific context is crucial for effective data-driven discovery.

The Signal-to-Noise Ratio: Quantifying Clarity in Complex Systems

The signal-to-noise ratio (SNR) is a fundamental concept in information theory and data analysis, but it is frequently misunderstood or oversimplified in practical applications. SNR is a quantitative measure of how much meaningful information (signal) exists in relation to irrelevant or interfering information (noise) in a given dataset or communication channel. However, the practical application of this concept in complex data analysis scenarios necessitates a more nuanced understanding that extends far beyond basic mathematical formulas.

In its original engineering context, signal-to-noise ratio was simple to define and quantify. When transmitting a radio signal, for example, the signal consists of the intentional electromagnetic waves carrying information, whereas noise consists of random electromagnetic interference various sources. The ratio between the power of the intended signal and the power of the interfering noise provides a clear measure of communication quality.

However, when we attempt to apply this concept to complex data analysis scenarios, the definition of both signal and noise becomes much more subjective and context dependent. What constitutes a signal depends entirely on what questions we're trying to answer, what decisions we're trying to make, and what phenomena we're trying to understand. Similarly, what constitutes noise depends on what we consider irrelevant to our current analytical purposes.

This subjectivity doesn't make the concept less valuable; quite the opposite. It makes the signal-to-noise ratio a powerful framework for thinking about the quality and utility of different data sources, analytical approaches, and conclusions. But it does mean that we must be explicit about how we're defining signal and noise in any particular context.

Consider the challenge of using customer behavior data to forecast future purchasing patterns. In this context, a signal could be consistent patterns in customer responses to various products, prices, or marketing messages. Noise can include random variations in individual behavior, temporary external influences such as weather or news events, or systematic biases in data collection. However, the definitions of signal and noise may change if our goal shifts from predicting purchasing patterns to understanding customer satisfaction. Patterns that were once signals for prediction may become noise for satisfaction analysis, and vice versa. One of the most important insights about signal-to-noise ratios in complex systems is that they are not fixed dataset properties; rather, they are heavily influenced by how we choose to analyze and interpret our data. The same dataset may have a very high SNR for one type of analysis but a very low SNR for another. This insight has far-reaching implications for how we approach data analysis and evaluate the efficacy of various analytical approaches. The temporal dimension of signal-to-noise ratios adds an extra layer of complexity. In many systems, signal strength varies over time, sometimes predictably, sometimes unpredictably. Economic indicators may have high signal-to-noise ratios during stable periods but significantly lower ratios during times of crisis or transition. Understanding temporal variations is critical for developing robust analytical systems. Similarly, the scale at which we analyze data can dramatically affect signal-to-noise ratios. Patterns that are invisible at one level of aggregation might become clear at another level. Individual customer transactions might appear noisy and unpredictable, but when aggregated by customer segment or time period, clear patterns might emerge. Conversely, patterns that are apparent in aggregate data might obscure important variations at more granular levels. The concept of effective signal-to-noise ratio takes into account not just the raw ratio of signal to noise, but also our ability to detect and extract the available signal using our current analytical methods. Two datasets might have identical raw signal-to-noise ratios, but if we have better methods for extracting signal from one than from the other, the effective SNR will be different.

This perspective emphasizes the importance of methodological sophistication in data analysis. Advanced statistical techniques, machine learning algorithms, and domain-specific analytical approaches can often extract signal from data that appears hopelessly noisy when analyzed with simpler methods. The history of data analysis is largely a history of developing increasingly sophisticated methods for improving effective signal-to-noise ratios. However, there are fundamental limits to how much signal can be extracted from any given dataset, and understanding these limits is crucial for setting appropriate expectations and making sound decisions about resource allocation. The theoretical maximum signal-to-noise ratio for any dataset is determined by the underlying phenomena being studied and the quality of data collection methods. No amount of analytical sophistication can extract signal that simply isn't there. The practical implications of signal-to-noise ratios extend far beyond technical considerations to fundamental questions about decision-making under uncertainty. When signal-to-noise ratios are high, we can make decisions with confidence based on data analysis. When ratios are low, we must be more cautious about drawing strong conclusions and should consider alternative approaches to decision-making. Understanding signal-to-noise ratios also helps us make better decisions about data collection and experimental design. If we know that certain types of data tend to have low signal-to-noise ratios, we can design our data collection efforts to maximize signal and minimize noise. This might involve collecting larger samples, using more precise measurement instruments, controlling for confounding variables, or changing the timing or context of data collection.

The concept of signal-to-noise ratio also provides a framework for thinking about the value of information. Information with high signal-to-noise ratios is generally more valuable than information with low ratios, all else being equal. This insight can help organizations prioritize their data collection and analysis efforts, focusing resources on sources and types of analysis that are likely to yield the highest-quality insights. In complex organizational contexts, different stakeholders might have different definitions of what constitutes signal versus noise, leading to disagreements about the interpretation of analytical results. Making these definitions explicit and ensuring alignment among stakeholders is crucial for effective data-driven decision-making. The emergence of big data and advanced analytics has created new opportunities for improving signal-to-noise ratios through techniques like ensemble methods, which combine multiple analytical approaches to extract more signal than any single approach could achieve. These techniques recognize that different methods might be sensitive to different aspects of the underlying signal and that combining multiple perspectives can yield more robust insights. However, the availability of large datasets and powerful analytical tools has also created new challenges for managing signal-to-noise ratios. The curse of dimensionality means that as we measure more and more variables, the probability of finding spurious patterns increases. The key is developing analytical approaches that can distinguish between genuine signals and patterns that arise simply from having too many variables relative to the amount of true signal in the data.

3

THE ARCHITECTURE OF DISCOVERY DESIGNING SYSTEMS FOR INSIGHT

The metaphor of architecture is particularly apt when discussing the systematic approach to data-driven discovery. Just as physical architecture entails creating structures that are both functional and beautiful, information architecture entails creating systems and processes that allow data to flow from its raw state to actionable insights. The best information architectures are invisible to their users; they facilitate discovery in such a natural and efficient manner that the underlying complexity is hidden. Understanding the landscape of questions that an organization or individual must answer is the first step toward creating effective information architecture. This landscape is dynamic; it changes as businesses expand, markets shift, and new opportunities and challenges arise. The architecture must be adaptable enough to accommodate this evolution while remaining structured enough to provide dependable, consistent paths to insight. The "ontology of inquiry" is a systematic understanding of the types of questions that are most important, how those questions relate to one another, and what types of evidence are required to effectively answer them. This ontology provides a framework for developing data collection systems, analytical processes, and communication mechanisms. Consider a retail company attempting to understand customer behavior. The ontology of the inquiry could include questions about customer acquisition (how do customers find our products? What channels work best for different customer segments?), customer experience (what factors influence satisfaction? Where do customers experience friction on their journey?), and customer lifetime value (How do we identify high-value customers? What interventions improve retention? Each of these question categories necessitates a different type of data, analytical approach, and method of presenting insights. The information architecture must meet all of these requirements while also ensuring that insights from various areas can be integrated as needed. One of the most important aspects of information architecture is the creation of feedback loops that allow the system to learn and improve with time. Traditional reporting systems frequently operate in a one-way flow: data comes in, reports go out, and there is little mechanism for determining whether the reports resulted in better decisions. Modern information architectures incorporate mechanisms for tracking how insights are used, what decisions they influence, and what outcomes result from those decisions. These feedback loops serve multiple purposes. They help identify which types of analysis are most valuable and should be prioritized. They reveal gaps in the current architecture where important questions are not being adequately addressed. They provide evidence about the effectiveness of different analytical approaches. And they create a learning culture where the value of data-driven insights is continuously reinforced.

The concept of "progressive disclosure" from user interface design is also relevant to information architecture. Not all users need access to all information at all times. Different roles, different decision contexts, and different levels of expertise require different presentations of the same underlying information. Effective information architecture provides multiple pathways to insight, allowing users to start with high-level summaries and drill down to more detailed analysis as needed. For example, a company's executive dashboard might present key performance indicators at a very high level, with the ability to click through to more detailed analyses. Operational managers might need more granular, real-time information about specific processes. Analysts might need access to raw data and sophisticated analytical tools. The architecture must serve all of these needs without overwhelming any particular user group with irrelevant information. The temporal dimension of information architecture is often overlooked but critically important. Different types of decisions require information at different time horizons and with different update frequencies. Strategic decisions might require analysis of long-term trends updated monthly or quarterly. Operational decisions might require real-time or near-real-time information. The architecture must be designed to support both requirements efficiently. Moreover, the architecture must account for the fact that the value and relevance of information change over time. Historical data that was once crucial for understanding trends might become less relevant as business conditions change. The system must provide mechanisms for archiving, summarizing, or discarding information that is no longer needed while preserving information that might become valuable again in the future. Data lineage and provenance represent another crucial aspect of information architecture. Users need to understand where information comes from, how it has been processed, and what limitations or assumptions are built into the analysis. This transparency is essential not only for technical accuracy but also for building trust in data-driven insights. Effective data lineage documentation serves multiple purposes. It helps users understand the appropriate uses and limitations of different information. It enables troubleshooting when results seem unexpected or incorrect. It facilitates compliance with regulatory requirements. And it supports reproducibility, allowing analyses to be repeated or modified as needed. The social architecture of information systems is just as important as the technical architecture. Data-driven insights are most valuable when they can be easily shared, discussed, and acted upon by multiple stakeholders. This requires designing not just technical systems but also social processes that encourage collaboration, knowledge sharing, and collective learning. This might involve creating regular forums for sharing interesting findings, establishing processes for cross-functional analysis projects, or developing training programs that help non-technical stakeholders understand and contribute to analytical efforts. The goal is to create a culture where data-driven insights flow naturally throughout the organization and where diverse perspectives contribute to better understanding. Scalability represents another fundamental consideration in information architecture design. Systems that work well for small amounts of data or small numbers of users may break down as scale increases. The architecture must be designed to handle growth in data volume, user base, and analytical complexity without requiring complete redesign. This scalability requirement affects every aspect of the architecture, from data storage and processing systems to analytical workflows to presentation mechanisms. It requires thinking carefully about which components are likely to become bottlenecks as the system grows and designing those components with appropriate flexibility and capacity.

Finally, effective information architecture must balance standardization with customization. Standardized approaches enable efficiency, consistency, and knowledge sharing across the organization. But different business units, different types of decisions, and different analytical challenges may require customized approaches. The architecture must provide a common foundation while allowing for appropriate variation and experimentation.

The Discovery Pipeline: From Raw Data to Actionable Intelligence

The transformation of raw data into actionable intelligence is a multi-stage process with unique challenges, requirements, and opportunities for success and failure. Understanding this pipeline, including its components, dependencies, and potential failure points, is critical for developing robust systems that consistently generate valuable insights. The discovery pipeline begins long before data collection starts. The first stage is what we might call "opportunity identification," which is the process of recognizing that a specific question or decision could benefit from data-driven analytics. This stage is frequently overlooked in discussions about data analysis, but it is critical for determining the overall value of the pipeline. Effective opportunity identification necessitates a mix of domain knowledge, analytical thinking, and organizational awareness. It entails determining which business problems are both significant enough to warrant analytical effort and appropriate for data-driven approaches. Data analysis cannot solve all important problems, and not all data-driven problems are worth the effort. Good analytical opportunities are typically defined by the availability of relevant data or the feasibility of collecting such data, the potential for insights to influence important decisions, the presence of stakeholders who are willing and able to act on analytical insights, and the absence of simpler, non-analytical approaches that could address the same problem more efficiently.

Once an opportunity has been identified, the next step is what we might call "analytical design," or the process of translating business questions into specific analytical approaches. This stage necessitates understanding not only what questions to ask, but also how to ask them in ways that can be answered using existing data and methods. Analytical design entails several important decisions: Which hypotheses should be tested? Which variables should be measured? Which analytical methods are most appropriate? How will the results be validated? How will the insights be communicated?

These decisions are interconnected and frequently necessitate iteration as our understanding of the problem and the available data grows. The data collection stage is where theoretical analysis designs encounter practical realities. Even when relevant data is already available, extracting, cleaning, and preparing it for analysis frequently reveals complications that were not anticipated during the design phase. Data may be stored in incompatible formats, contain errors or inconsistencies, or not measure what it was intended to measure. Modern data collection frequently requires combining information from multiple sources, each with its own format, quality characteristics, and limitations. This integration process is both technically difficult and conceptually complex, necessitating decisions about how to handle discrepancies between sources, align different measurement scales and definitions, and manage the temporal aspects of combining data collected at different times. The data preparation stage, also known as data wrangling or data munging, typically requires far more time and effort than initial analytical designs anticipate. This stage includes not only technical tasks like format conversion and error correction but also conceptual ones such as variable definition, outlier handling, and missing data management. Each of these decisions can have a significant impact on analytical results, but they are frequently made quickly and without careful consideration of their implications. Effective discovery pipelines include explicit decision-making processes for data preparation, such as documentation of choices and consideration of how different choices may affect results. The analytical modeling stage involves applying statistical techniques, machine learning algorithms, and other analytical methods to prepared data. This stage is frequently given the most attention in discussions about data analysis, but it is only one component of a larger pipeline. The quality of analytical modeling is heavily dependent on the quality of the preceding stages.

Effective analytical modeling involves not just applying techniques correctly, but also understanding their assumptions, limitations, and appropriate contexts for use. It requires iterating between different approaches, testing the robustness of results, and understanding how methodological choices affect conclusions. The validation stage involves testing whether analytical results are reliable, meaningful, and generalizable. This might involve statistical techniques for assessing the significance and robustness of findings, but it also involves broader questions about whether results make sense in light of domain expertise and whether they hold up under different assumptions or with different data. Validation is particularly important in the context of machine learning and other automated analytical techniques, which can sometimes produce results that are statistically sophisticated but practically meaningless. The validation stage serves as a crucial check against overfitting, spurious patterns, and other analytical pitfalls. The interpretation stage involves translating analytical results into meaningful insights that can inform decision-making. This stage requires not just understanding what the analysis shows, but also understanding what it doesn't show, what assumptions underlie the results, and how confident we should be in different conclusions. Effective interpretation requires close collaboration between analysts and domain experts. Analysts bring technical expertise about what different analytical results mean and how confident we should be in them. Domain experts bring contextual knowledge about what results are surprising, what results are consistent with other knowledge, and what results would be most important for decision-making. The communication stage involves presenting insights in ways that are accessible, compelling, and actionable for different stakeholder audiences. This requires understanding not just what the analysis shows, but also what different audiences need to know, what they already understand, and what kinds of presentations are most likely to influence their decisions. Effective communication often requires multiple presentations of the same insights, tailored for different audiences and different decision contexts. An analysis might be presented as a detailed technical report for other analysts, as an executive summary for senior management, and as a set of operational recommendations for front-line staff. The action stage involves translating insights into actual decisions and implementations. This stage is often beyond the direct control of analysts, but the entire value of the discovery pipeline depends on whether insights actually influence decisions and whether those decisions lead to better outcomes. Effective discovery pipelines include mechanisms for tracking how insights are used, what decisions they influence, and what outcomes result. This feedback is crucial for improving future iterations of the pipeline and for demonstrating the value of analytical efforts. The learning stage involves reflecting on the entire pipeline process to identify what worked well, what could be improved, and what lessons can be applied to future analytical projects. This meta-analytical process is essential for organizational learning and for continuous improvement of the discovery pipeline. Each stage of the discovery pipeline presents opportunities for both optimization and failure. Understanding these opportunities and designing processes that maximize the likelihood of success at each stage is essential for building organizational capabilities in data-driven discovery.

Feedback Loops: How Systems Learn and Adapt Over Time

The most sophisticated data analysis systems are not static tools but adaptive systems that improve their performance over time through systematic feedback loops. These feedback mechanisms transform one-time analytical projects into learning systems that become more effective, more efficient, and more valuable with each iteration. Understanding how to design and implement these feedback loops is crucial for building sustainable competitive advantages through data-driven discovery. Feedback loops in analytical systems operate at multiple levels and time scales. At the most immediate level, analysts receive feedback about their methods and conclusions through the process of peer review, stakeholder discussion, and results validation. This feedback helps improve the quality of individual analyses and helps analysts develop better instincts about which approaches are likely to be effective for different types of problems. At a project level, feedback loops involve tracking how analytical insights are received, understood, and acted upon by decision-makers. This feedback is crucial for understanding which types of analysis provide the most value, which presentation formats are most effective, and which analytical approaches are most trusted by different stakeholder groups. At an organizational level, feedback loops involve systematic assessment of how data-driven insights contribute to business outcomes. This might involve tracking the relationship between analytical recommendations and subsequent performance, monitoring the adoption rate of data-driven decision-making across different parts of the organization, or measuring the return on investment from analytical capabilities. The design of effective feedback loops requires careful consideration of what to measure, how to measure it, and how to use the resulting information to drive improvements. The measurements must be specific enough to provide actionable insights but broad enough to capture the full value that analytical systems provide. One of the most important types of feedback involves prediction accuracy. When analytical systems make predictions about future events, the accuracy of those predictions provides clear feedback about the quality of the underlying models and methods. This feedback can be used to refine models, adjust parameters, and improve future predictions. However, prediction accuracy feedback is not always straightforward to implement. In many business contexts, the outcomes that matter most unfold over long time periods, making it difficult to provide timely feedback to analysts. Moreover, business decisions based on analytical insights may change the very outcomes that the analysis was trying to predict, creating complications in assessing prediction accuracy. Decision quality feedback involves assessing whether decisions informed by analytical insights lead to better outcomes than decisions made through other approaches. This type of feedback is particularly valuable because it directly addresses the ultimate purpose of the most analytical effort: improving decision-making.

Measuring decision quality requires establishing appropriate comparison groups and controlling other factors that might influence outcomes. This can be challenging in business contexts where it may not be feasible or ethical to randomly assign some decisions to be made with analytical support and others without such support. Process efficiency feedback involves tracking how analytical systems perform in terms of speed, cost, and resource utilization. This feedback is important for ensuring that analytical capabilities remain cost-effective and for identifying opportunities to improve efficiency without sacrificing quality. Process efficiency feedback might track metrics like the time required to complete different types of analyses, the cost per insight generated, or the ratio of analytical effort to business impact. These metrics help organizations optimize their analytical investments and identify areas where process improvements could yield significant benefits. User satisfaction feedback involves understanding how well analytical systems meet the needs and expectations of their users. This includes not just the accuracy and usefulness of analytical outputs, but also factors like ease of use, timeliness, and integration with existing workflows. User satisfaction feedback often reveals important gaps between what analytical systems are designed to provide and what users actually need. This feedback can guide improvements in system design, analytical methods, and communication approaches. Learning curved feedback involves tracking how quickly individuals and organizations develop competency in using analytical tools and interpreting analytical results. This feedback is particularly important as organizations scale their analytical capabilities and bring new users into the system. Understanding learning curves helps organizations design better training programs, identify where additional support is needed, and recognize when analytical approaches may be too complex for their intended users. The implementation of feedback loops requires not just measurement systems but also organizational processes for acting on the feedback received. This includes regular review meetings where feedback is discussed, systematic processes for prioritizing improvements, and mechanisms for tracking whether improvements actually lead to better outcomes. Effective feedback loops also require creating a culture where feedback is valued and where both positive and negative feedback are seen as opportunities for learning rather than as judgments about individual or organizational performance. This cultural dimension is often the most challenging aspect of implementing feedback systems. The temporal dimension of feedback loops is particularly important. Different types of feedback operate on different time scales; some provide immediate insights that can be acted upon quickly, while others require longer observation periods to generate meaningful insights. Designing systems that capture and utilize feedback at all relevant time scales is essential for comprehensive learning.

Feedback loops must also account for the fact that analytical systems exist within larger organizational and environmental contexts that are constantly changing. Feedback that was relevant and actionable at one point in time may become less relevant as business conditions, competitive landscapes, or organizational priorities change. This dynamic context means that feedback systems themselves must evolve over time. The metrics that matter most, the methods for collecting feedback, and the processes for acting on feedback all need to be regularly reviewed and updated to ensure they remain aligned with current needs and priorities. The goal of implementing comprehensive feedback loops is to create analytical systems that exhibit what we might call "collective intelligence “systems that become smarter and more effective through the accumulated experience of all their users and all their applications. These systems represent the pinnacle of data-driven discovery because they combine the best aspects of human judgment and machine capability in adaptive systems that continuously improve their ability to transform data into wisdom.

4

STATISTICAL THINKING THE MATHEMATICS OF UNCERTAINTY

Statistical thinking begins with the recognition that uncertainty is not a flaw in our analytical systems but rather a fundamental feature of the world we seek to comprehend. In most real-world situations, we cannot know the outcome with absolute certainty, forecast future events with perfect accuracy, or measure phenomena without some degree of error. Rather than viewing uncertainty as a constraint, statistical thinking sees it as a source of information that can be quantified, analyzed, and incorporated into decision-making processes. Probability theory provides the mathematical foundation for systematically addressing uncertainty. However, in order to use probability effectively in data-driven discovery, we must first recognize it as a language for expressing and reasoning about uncertain beliefs and incomplete knowledge, rather than simply a mathematical formalism. This language allows us to express what we know and don't know, to update our beliefs as new evidence becomes available, and to make decisions based on all possible outcomes. The most fundamental principle of probabilistic thinking is that uncertainty can be quantified. Instead of simply stating that we are "uncertain" about something, we can quantify our degree of uncertainty. This quantification enables us to compare various sources of uncertainty, combine data from multiple sources, and make decisions that best reflect what we know and don't know. Consider the challenge of medical diagnosis. A physician examining a patient with certain symptoms cannot be absolutely certain about the underlying condition, but probabilistic thinking allows her to quantify the likelihood of different diagnoses based on the available evidence. Test results, patient history, and clinical observations all provide information that can be combined using probability theory to estimate the likelihood of different conditions. This probabilistic approach to diagnosis is not only more precise than intuitive approaches, but it also provides a framework for incorporating new data as it becomes available. If new test results become available, Bayesian reasoning offers a systematic method for updating probability estimates for various diagnoses. The concept of probability distributions is one of the most powerful tools in the probabilistic toolbox. Rather than viewing uncertain quantities as having a single unknown value, probability distributions allow us to characterize the entire range of possible values and their relative likelihoods. This viewpoint provides much more information than point estimates and allows for more sophisticated reasoning about uncertainty.

For example, when forecasting sales for the next quarter, a probabilistic approach might define the forecast as a probability distribution that shows not only the most likely outcome but also the full range of plausible outcomes given available information. This distribution may indicate that, while 5% growth is the most likely outcome, there is a significant chance of a 10% decline or a 20% increase. This distributional perspective has important implications for decision-making. Decisions that appear optimal based on expected values may appear much less appealing when the entire distribution of possible outcomes is considered. Understanding the tails of probability distributions, or low-probability but high-impact events, is frequently required for making sound decisions. The concept of conditional probability represents another crucial element of probabilistic thinking. Most real-world probabilities are conditional; they depend on what else we know or assume about the situation. Recognizing and correctly handling these conditional relationships is essential for accurate probabilistic reasoning. Consider the challenge of fraud detection in financial transactions. The probability that any given transaction is fraudulent is very low, perhaps one in a thousand. But the probability of fraud becomes much higher when we condition on certain characteristics of the transaction: unusual amounts, unusual timing, unusual locations, or patterns that deviate from the customer's typical behavior. Effective fraud detection systems work by computing conditional probabilities; they estimate the probability of fraud given all available information about the transaction and the customer. This conditional approach allows them to identify potentially fraudulent transactions while minimizing false alarms. The law of total probability provides a framework for thinking about complex situations involving multiple possible scenarios. When there are several different ways that an event could occur, the total probability of that event is the sum of the probabilities of each pathway, weighted by the probability of the conditions that lead to each pathway. This principle is particularly useful in business forecasting, where outcomes often depend on multiple uncertain factors. Sales forecasts might depend on economic conditions, competitive actions, and internal execution, each of which is uncertain. The law of total probability provides a systematic method for combining these different sources of uncertainty into an overall forecast. Independence and correlation represent fundamental concepts that are often misunderstood in practical applications. Two events are independent if knowing about one provides no information about the other. Many probabilistic calculations assume independence, but this assumption is frequently violated in real-world situations, leading to incorrect conclusions. For example, the assumption that different market risks are independent has contributed to several financial crises. During periods of market stress, risks that appear independent under normal conditions often become highly correlated, leading to simultaneous failures across different sectors or regions. Understanding when independence assumptions are reasonable and when they are likely to be violated is crucial for accurate probabilistic reasoning. This understanding often requires deep domain expertise rather than just mathematical sophistication. The principle of expected value provides a bridge between probabilistic thinking and decision-making. The expected value of an uncertain quantity is the average outcome we would expect if we could repeat the situation many times. While any single outcome might differ from the expected value, decisions based on expected values tend to perform well over multiple repetitions.

That said, expected value decision-making has important limitations. It may not be appropriate when individual outcomes have vastly different utilities, when we care about worst-case scenarios, or when we are dealing with rare but high-impact events. Understanding when expected value reasoning is appropriate and when other decision criteria should be used is an important aspect of probabilistic thinking. The Monte Carlo method represents one of the most powerful computational tools for probabilistic reasoning. When analytical solutions are impossible or impractical, Monte Carlo simulation allows us to explore the behavior of complex probabilistic systems by generating many random scenarios and observing the patterns that emerge. Monte Carlo methods are particularly valuable for understanding the behavior of complex systems where multiple sources of uncertainty interact in complicated ways. Rather than trying to solve complex mathematical equations, we can simulate thousands or millions of possible scenarios and observe the distribution of outcomes. Probabilistic thinking also provides a framework for thinking about the quality of information and the value of additional data. Information theory, which grew out of probability theory, provides tools for quantifying how much information is provided by different observations and for understanding when additional data collection is likely to be valuable. This perspective is crucial for making good decisions about where to invest analytical resources. Some additional data might provide very little new information, while other data might dramatically change our understanding of a situation. Probabilistic thinking provides tools for making these distinctions systematically.

Bayesian Reasoning: Updating Beliefs with New Evidence

Bayesian reasoning represents one of the most powerful and elegant frameworks for learning from data and updating beliefs in light of new evidence. Named after the 18th-century statistician Thomas Bayes, this approach provides a systematic method for incorporating new information into existing knowledge, making it particularly valuable for data-driven discovery in complex, evolving situations. The fundamental insight of Bayesian reasoning is that our beliefs about uncertain propositions should be expressed as probabilities and that these probabilities should be updated systematically as new evidence becomes available. This approach stands in contrast to traditional scientific thinking, which often treats hypotheses as either true or false, and to classical statistical methods, which focus primarily on rejecting null hypotheses rather than on quantifying degrees of belief. Bayes' theorem provides the mathematical foundation for this updating process. In its simplest form, the theorem shows how to compute the probability of a hypothesis after observing new evidence, based on the probability of the hypothesis before observing the evidence and the likelihood of observing that evidence under different possible hypotheses. This mathematical relationship might seem abstract, but it captures something fundamental about how rational thinking should work. When we encounter new information, we should neither ignore our previous knowledge nor ignore the new evidence. Instead, we should combine both sources of information in a way that gives appropriate weight to each.

Consider the example of medical testing. Suppose a patient tests positive for a rare disease that affects 1 in 1000 people. If the test is 99% accurate (correctly identifying 99% of people with the disease and correctly identifying 99% of people without the disease), what is the probability that the patient actually has the disease? Intuitive reasoning might suggest that the probability is very high; after all, the test is 99% accurate. But Bayesian reasoning reveals that the probability is actually much lower than most people would guess. Because the disease is rare, most positive test results are false positives, and the probability that the patient actually has the disease is only about 9%. This counterintuitive result illustrates the importance of considering base rates, the prior probability of different hypotheses, before new evidence is observed. When diseases are rare, tests have high false positive rates, and when phenomena are common, we should be more confident in positive results. Prior probabilities are central to Bayesian reasoning and often controversial in practical applications. Critics argue that prior probabilities are subjective and that different people might reasonably have different priors for the same situation. Proponents argue that prior probabilities simply make explicit the background assumptions that are implicit in any reasoning process. In practice, the choice of prior probabilities often matters less than critics suggest, especially when substantial evidence is available. As more evidence accumulates, the influence of prior probabilities diminish, and conclusions tend to converge regardless of reasonable differences in initial beliefs. This property, known as the washing, out of priors, suggests that Bayesian reasoning becomes more objective as more data becomes available.

However, the choice of priors can be crucial when evidence is limited or when dealing with rare events. In these situations, careful consideration of what prior probabilities are reasonable becomes an important part of the analytical process. This consideration often requires domain expertise and careful thinking about what background knowledge is relevant. Sequential updating represents one of the most powerful aspects of Bayesian reasoning. Rather than treating each piece of evidence in isolation, Bayesian methods allow us to incorporate evidence sequentially, with each new observation updating our beliefs and providing the starting point for interpreting the next observation. This sequential approach is particularly valuable in dynamic situations where new information becomes available continuously. Rather than waiting to collect all possible evidence before drawing conclusions, we can update our understanding continuously as new information arrives. Consider the challenge of monitoring the performance of a new product launch. Traditional approaches might wait for complete quarterly results before assessing performance. A Bayesian approach would continuously update estimates of product performance as daily or weekly sales data becomes available, providing more timely insights for decision-making. The conjugate priors provide computational advantages in certain Bayesian analyses. When the prior probability distribution belongs to the same family as the likelihood function, the posterior distribution (after updating with evidence) belongs to the same family as the prior. This mathematical convenience makes Bayesian updating computationally tractable in many situations. While conjugate priors are mathematically convenient, they may not always represent the most realistic assumptions about prior knowledge. Modern computational methods, particularly Markov Chain Monte Carlo (MCMC) techniques, have made it possible to use more realistic prior distributions even when they don't have convenient mathematical properties. Bayesian model comparison provides a framework for choosing between different hypotheses or models based on their ability to explain observed data. Rather than simply testing whether individual models fit the data adequately, Bayesian comparison considers how well different models predict the observed data, naturally accounting for model complexity and the risk of overfitting. This approach is particularly valuable when multiple explanations for the same phenomenon are plausible. Rather than being forced to choose a single "correct" model, Bayesian methods allow us to quantify our confidence in different models and even to average across models when appropriate.

Hierarchical Bayesian models represent a sophisticated extension of basic Bayesian reasoning that is particularly useful for analyzing data with natural grouping structures. These models allow for sharing information across related groups while still accounting for differences between groups. For example, in analyzing customer behavior across different market segments, a hierarchical Bayesian model might assume that behavior within each segment follows similar patterns but that the specific parameters of those patterns differ across segments. This approach allows the model to learn from the overall patterns across all segments while still capturing segment-specific differences. The empirical Bayes approach provides a compromise between fully Bayesian methods and classical statistical approaches. In empirical Bayes, prior distributions are estimated from the data itself rather than being specified based on external knowledge. This approach can provide some of the benefits of Bayesian reasoning while avoiding some of the controversies about subjective priors. Bayesian reasoning also provides a natural framework for incorporating expert knowledge and qualitative information into quantitative analyses. Expert opinions can be formalized as prior distributions, allowing quantitative and qualitative information to be combined systematically. This integration is particularly valuable in situations where historical data is limited but expert knowledge is available. Rather than ignoring expert knowledge because it cannot be easily quantified, Bayesian methods provide tools for incorporating such knowledge appropriately. The computational revolution has made Bayesian methods much more practical for real-world applications. Modern software packages provide user-friendly interfaces for specifying and fitting Bayesian models, making these powerful methods accessible to practitioners who are not specialists in Bayesian statistics. However, the increased accessibility of Bayesian methods also creates new challenges. Users must understand not just how to use the software, but also how to specify appropriate models, how to choose reasonable prior distributions, and how to interpret results correctly. The flexibility of Bayesian methods means that inappropriate applications can lead to misleading conclusions. Despite these challenges, Bayesian reasoning provides one of the most coherent and powerful frameworks available for learning from data and making decisions under uncertainty. Its emphasis on updating beliefs systematically as new evidence becomes available aligns closely with the goals of data-driven discovery and provides a principled approach to the inevitable uncertainties that characterize most real-world analytical challenges.

The Power of Distributions: Understanding Variability and Central Tendencies

The theory of probability distributions is a fundamental component of statistical analysis, providing a comprehensive framework for understanding data. While many practitioners rely heavily on summary statistics like means, medians, and standard deviations, they frequently provide a limited view of a dataset. The emphasis on the full distribution shifts the analytical lens from isolated values to a more comprehensive view of variability, allowing for a better understanding of data's underlying structure and behavior.

A probability distribution does more than just identify potential values for a variable; it also describes the likelihood of each outcome. This breadth enables analysts to investigate not only what is typical, but also what is feasible and how those possibilities are distributed. For example, while a dataset's mean may indicate a central tendency, it does not provide information about the spread or probability of extreme events. The distribution's shape, whether symmetric, skewed, unimodal, or multimodal, contains important information about the processes that generate the data. In practice, this means that two datasets can have the same meaning and variance but fundamentally different distributions, resulting in very different stories about the phenomena they represent. Consider the example of income data, which is notoriously skewed in most societies. Reporting only the average income may paint an inaccurate picture of overall prosperity if a small percentage of high earners significantly inflates that average. A distributional analysis, on the other hand, shows the entire range of incomes, highlighting inequality, identifying clusters or gaps, and determining whether the distribution has long tails or significant outliers. This type of insight is critical for developing effective policies or making informed business decisions because it aligns data analysis with the real-world complexity it seeks to comprehend. Finally, distributed thinking improves statistical practice. It enables analysts and decision-makers to move beyond reductive summaries and engage with the nuanced, and often messy, variability that data brings. This results in a more honest and powerful lens for interpreting the world through numbers.

5

COGNITIVE BIASES AND MENTAL MODELS THE HUMAN ELEMENT IN DATA

Data analysis is often perceived as an objective, mechanical process where numbers speak for themselves and conclusions emerge naturally from statistical procedures. This perception, however, fundamentally misunderstands the deep human nature of analytical work. Every step of the data analysis process, from the initial framing of questions to the final interpretation of results, is filtered through the lens of human cognition with all its remarkable capabilities and systematic limitations. The human mind, evolved over millennia to make rapid decisions in uncertain environments, employs a sophisticated array of mental shortcuts and pattern recognition systems. These cognitive mechanisms served our ancestors well when quick judgments meant the difference between survival and death, but they can lead us astray in the context of modern data analysis where precision, objectivity, and systematic thinking are paramount. Understanding these cognitive tendencies is not merely an academic exercise but a practical necessity for anyone seeking to extract meaningful insights from data.

The intersection of human psychology and data analysis creates a complex landscape where statistical rigor meets cognitive fallibility. This chapter explores how our mental architecture both enables and constrains our ability to understand data, examining the systematic biases that can distort our analytical processes and introducing frameworks for building more reliable mental models of the phenomena we study.

The Confirmation Trap: How Preconceptions Distort Analysis

The human tendency to seek information that confirms existing beliefs while avoiding or dismissing contradictory evidence represents perhaps the most pervasive and dangerous bias in data analysis. Confirmation bias operates at multiple levels, from the conscious selection of data sources that support predetermined conclusions to the unconscious weighting of evidence that aligns with our expectations. Consider the analyst tasked with evaluating the effectiveness of a new marketing campaign. If the analyst begins with the belief that the campaign will be successful, perhaps due to personal investment in its design or pressure from management, this preconception subtly influences every subsequent analytical decision. The choice of metrics becomes skewed toward those likely to show positive results. Time periods are selected and exclude potentially confounding factors. Comparison groups are chosen that maximize the apparent impact of the intervention. This selective attention extends beyond conscious decision-making into the realm of perception itself. When examining visualizations or summary statistics, analysts literally see patterns differently based on their expectations. A scatter plot showing a weak positive correlation might be interpreted as strong evidence of causation by someone expecting such a relationship, while the same plot might be dismissed as noise by someone with contrary expectations. The data remains identical, but the cognitive processing transforms it into entirely different conclusions. The confirmation trap becomes particularly insidious in exploratory data analysis, where the absence of predetermined hypotheses might seem to provide protection against bias. Instead, it creates an environment where the analyst can unconsciously select from an enormous number of possible patterns and relationships, gravitating toward those that align with emerging preconceptions or that tell compelling stories. The sheer volume of potential analyses in large datasets means that statistically significant relationships will emerge by chance alone, and confirmation bias leads analysts to preferentially pursue and elaborate on those that feel intuitively correct. Professional data analysts are not immune to these tendencies despite their training and awareness. The pressure to produce actionable insights, combined with organizational cultures that reward confident conclusions over uncertain explorations, creates powerful incentives to find patterns and relationships even when they may not exist or may be far weaker than they appear. The analyst who consistently reports ambiguous or negative results may find their credibility questioned, while those who discover clear, actionable insights are celebrated regardless of the robustness of their underlying analysis. The temporal aspect of confirmation bias adds another layer of complexity. Initial findings, even preliminary ones, establish cognitive anchors that influence all subsequent analysis. The first pattern noticed in a dataset takes on disproportionate importance, shaping the questions asked and the methods employed in further investigation. This anchoring effect means that the order in which analyses are conducted can fundamentally alter the final conclusions, even when using identical data and methods. Organizational dynamics amplify individual confirmation biases through groupthink and hierarchical pressures. When teams share common assumptions or when junior analysts understand what results are expected by senior leadership, the collective analytical process becomes systematically biased toward confirming organizational beliefs. The appearance of rigorous analysis may mask a process that was never truly open to discovering contrary evidence. The digital tools commonly used in data analysis inadvertently contribute to confirmation bias through their design and default behaviors. Statistical software packages that automatically highlight significant results, visualization tools that emphasize dramatic patterns, and machine learning platforms that optimize for performance metrics can all nudge analysts toward conclusions that feel satisfying but may not reflect the underlying reality of the data. Breaking free from the confirmation trap requires more than individual awareness or good intentions. It demands systematic approaches that structure the analytical process to actively seek disconfirming evidence and challenge initial assumptions. This might involve deliberately constructing alternative hypotheses and testing them with equal rigor, seeking out datasets or time periods that might contradict initial findings, or adopting analytical protocols that require explicit consideration of contrary evidence before reaching conclusions. The practice of red team analysis, borrowed from military and intelligence contexts, offers one approach to institutionalizing skepticism within analytical processes. By formally assigning team members to argue against emerging conclusions or to construct alternative interpretations of the same data, organizations can create systematic challenges to confirmation bias. This adversarial approach transforms what is often an unconscious bias into an explicit analytical consideration.

Availability Heuristics: When Recent Examples Overshadow the Whole

The human mind's tendency to judge the probability and importance of events based on how easily examples come to mind profoundly shapes how we interpret data and draw conclusions from analysis. This availability heuristic, while often useful in daily life, can dramatically distort our understanding of patterns and trends when applied uncritically to data analysis.

Recent events carry disproportionate weight in human cognition, creating a recency bias that can overshadow long-term trends and historical patterns. An analyst examining customer behavior data collected over several years might find their interpretation heavily influenced by a recent unusual event, such as a viral social media campaign or an economic disruption. The vivid, easily recalled recent experience becomes the lens through which all other data is interpreted, potentially obscuring more fundamental and stable patterns that would be revealed by a more systematic analysis. The media and communication environment in which analysts operate amplifies the availability heuristic by constantly highlighting dramatic, unusual, or recent events while underrepresenting routine, stable patterns. A data scientist studying market trends might overweight the importance of recently reported competitive moves or regulatory changes simply because they are top-of-mind, while failing to give adequate consideration to slower-moving demographic or technological shifts that may have far greater long-term impact. This bias toward the available and memorable creates systematic distortions in how we frame analytical questions and interpret results. Rare but memorable events receive attention disproportionate to their actual frequency or impact, while common but unremarkable patterns remain underexplored. The analyst studying product defects might focus extensively on a recent high-profile failure while neglecting to investigate the more numerous but less dramatic quality issues that collectively have a greater impact on customer satisfaction. The availability heuristic interacts with organizational culture and communication patterns in ways that can systematically skew analytical priorities. Events that generate internal discussion, media coverage, or executive attention become cognitively available to analysts, influencing their choice of research questions and their interpretation of results. Meanwhile, issues that affect large numbers of customers or generate significant business impact but fail to create memorable incidents may remain analytically underexplored.

Personal experience plays a particularly powerful role in making certain types of patterns and explanations cognitively available. An analyst who has previously encountered a particular type of data quality issue or who has experience with certain customer segments may interpret new data through the lens of these familiar examples. While experience can provide valuable insights, it can also create blind spots where patterns that don't match familiar templates are overlooked or misinterpreted. The structure of data itself can contribute to availability bias when certain types of information are more accessible or easier to analyze than others. Recent data is often completer and more accurate than historical information, leading analysts to weight recent patterns more heavily not just because they are psychologically available but because they are practically easier to work with. Similarly, data from systems with better logging or measurement capabilities may receive disproportionate attention compared to equally important but less well-documented phenomena. Seasonal and cyclical patterns create particularly complex interactions with availability bias. An analyst examining data during an unusual period may interpret temporary fluctuations as indicative of fundamental changes, while someone analyzing the same phenomenon during a typical period might miss important signals of emerging trends. The cognitive availability of the current context overwhelms the systematic consideration of longer-term patterns and cycles. The collaborative nature of much analytical work means that availability bias can be amplified through social processes. Team members share their most memorable experiences and recent insights, creating a collective pool of available examples that may not be representative of the broader phenomenon under study. These shared narratives and examples become the common framework through which the team interprets new data, potentially creating systematic blind spots where important patterns don't match the collectively available mental models. Visualization and reporting practices can either exacerbate or mitigate the effects of availability bias. Charts and graphs that emphasize recent time periods or dramatic changes make certain patterns more cognitively available while potentially obscuring longer-term trends. Conversely, visualizations that systematically present multiple time scales or that highlight base rates, and historical context can help counteract the natural tendency to outweigh recent or memorable events. The dynamic nature of many business and social phenomena means that the availability heuristic can create feedback loops that distort both analysis and decision-making. When analysts focus on recently available examples, their recommendations may address symptoms rather than root causes, leading to interventions that create new memorable events without resolving underlying issues. These new events then become cognitively available, potentially perpetuating a cycle of reactive analysis and decision-making. Overcoming availability bias requires systematic approaches that expand the range of examples and patterns that analysts consider. This might involve establishing analytical protocols that explicitly require consideration of historical precedents, base rates, and alternative time frames before drawing conclusions. Organizations can develop practices of maintaining case libraries or pattern databases that make a broader range of examples readily available to analysts, counteracting the natural tendency to rely on whatever happens to be top-of-mind. The practice of scenario analysis offers another approach to mitigating availability bias by systematically considering a range of possible explanations and outcomes rather than focusing only on those that are immediately obvious or memorable. By deliberately constructing alternative scenarios based on different assumptions or historical precedents, analysts can expand their consideration beyond the cognitively available examples that might otherwise dominate their thinking.

Regular rotation of analytical assignments and cross-training between different domains can help analysts develop a broader base of available examples and patterns, reducing the likelihood that their analysis will be overly influenced by a narrow range of recent or memorable experiences. This diversity of experience creates a richer set of cognitive resources that can be drawn upon when interpreting new data and patterns.

Constructing Better Mental Models: Tools for Clear Thinking

Mental models serve as the cognitive frameworks through which we understand and interpret data, shaping everything from the questions we ask to the conclusions we draw. These internal representations of how systems work, how variables relate to each other, and how patterns emerge over time are essential tools for making sense of complex information. However, the mental models we unconsciously employ in data analysis are often incomplete, inconsistent, or simply wrong, leading to systematic errors in interpretation and flawed decision-making. The construction of effective mental models requires deliberate effort and systematic approaches that go beyond intuitive understanding. A mental model is more than just a collection of facts or a simple cause-and-effect relationship; it is a dynamic, interconnected representation of how a system behaves under different conditions, how various components interact with each other, and how changes in one area ripple through the entire system. Consider the challenge of building a mental model for customer behavior in an e-commerce environment. A naive model might suggest that lower prices directly lead to higher sales, but a more sophisticated model must account for the complex relationships between price, perceived quality, brand positioning, competitive dynamics, seasonal patterns, economic conditions, and individual customer preferences. The quality of analytical insights depends directly on how well the underlying mental model captures these multifaceted relationships. The process of model construction begins with explicit articulation of assumptions and beliefs about the system under study. Many analytical errors stem from implicit assumptions that are never examined or tested. By forcing ourselves to write down what we believe about how a system works, we create opportunities to identify gaps, inconsistencies, and untested assumptions that might otherwise remain hidden. This articulation process often reveals that our intuitive understanding is far less complete or coherent than we initially believed. Systems thinking provides a powerful framework for constructing more robust mental models by emphasizing the relationships and feedback loops that connect different components of complex systems. Rather than focusing on individual variables or isolated cause-and-effect relationships, systems thinking encourages us to consider how changes propagate through networks of interconnected elements, how feedback loops can amplify or dampen certain effects, and how delays between causes and effects can make patterns difficult to recognize. The stock and flow dynamics offers particularly valuable insights for building mental models of business and social phenomena. Stocks represent the accumulated state of a system at any point in time, such as the number of customers, the level of brand awareness, or the amount of technical debt in a software system. Flows represent the rates at which these stocks change over time, such as customer acquisition rates, marketing investment, or code development velocity. Understanding these dynamics helps analysts recognize that many business problems involve managing the relationship between stocks and flows rather than simply optimizing individual metrics. Feedback loops represent another crucial element of effective mental models, helping analysts understand how actions and outcomes influence each other over time. Reinforcing feedback loops create virtuous or vicious cycles where initial changes are amplified, while balancing feedback loops create stability and resistance to change. An e-commerce platform that improves its search functionality may create a reinforcing loop where better search results lead to higher customer satisfaction, which leads to more positive reviews, which attracts more customers, which provides more data for further improving search functionality. The temporal dimension of mental models requires particular attention because many analytical errors stem from misunderstanding how patterns develop and change over time. Linear thinking assumes that effects are proportional to causes and that changes occur at constant rates, but real systems often exhibit exponential growth, threshold effects, cyclical patterns, and complex lag relationships. A robust mental model must account for these temporal complexities, including the possibility that the same action might have different effects depending on timing, context, and the current state of the system.

Mental models must also incorporate uncertainty and variability rather than assuming deterministic relationships between variables. Real systems are influenced by random events, measurement errors, and factors that are not included in our models. Effective mental models acknowledge this uncertainty explicitly, considering ranges of possible outcomes rather than point predictions and recognizing that apparent patterns might be due to chance rather than underlying causal relationships. The practice of model comparison offers a systematic approach to improving mental models by considering multiple alternative explanations for observed patterns. Rather than settling on the first plausible explanation for a set of data, analysts can construct several competing models and evaluate their relative strengths and weaknesses. This comparison process often reveals assumptions and limitations that are not apparent when considering only a single model. Analogical reasoning provides another tool for mental model construction by drawing insights from well-understood systems and applying them to less familiar domains. The key to effective analogical reasoning is identifying the appropriate level of abstraction where the analogy holds while remaining aware of the ways in which the analogy breaks down. An analyst studying viral marketing campaigns might draw insights from epidemiological models of disease transmission but must be careful not to assume that all aspects of disease dynamics apply to information spread. The iterative refinement of mental models through experience and feedback creates opportunities for continuous improvement in analytical thinking. Each new dataset and each analytical project provides evidence that can confirm, modify, or contradict aspects of our existing mental models. The willingness to update and revise models in response to new evidence distinguishes effective analysts from those who become trapped by their initial assumptions. Collaborative model building can help overcome the limitations of individual perspective by bringing together diverse viewpoints and experiences. When team members make their mental models explicit and compare them with others, the resulting discussion often reveals important assumptions and blind spots that no single person would have identified. This collaborative process can lead to more robust and comprehensive models that incorporate insights from multiple domains and perspectives. The documentation and sharing of mental models within organizations creates opportunities for collective learning and improvement. When successful mental models are captured and made available to other analysts, it accelerates the development of analytical capabilities across the organization. Conversely, the documentation of failed or flawed models provides valuable learning opportunities that can help others avoid similar pitfalls. The integration of quantitative and qualitative approaches to model building ensures that mental models remain grounded in both empirical evidence and practical understanding. While data analysis provides objective information about patterns and relationships, qualitative insights from domain experts, stakeholders, and direct observation help ensure that models capture the nuanced realities of how systems actually work in practice.

6

VISUALIZATION AND COMMUNICATION MAKING THE INVISIBLE VISIBLE

Data visualization stands at the intersection of art and science, transforming abstract numbers into visual forms that can be perceived, understood, and acted upon by human decision-makers. The power of visualization lies not merely in its ability to display information but in its capacity to reveal patterns, relationships, and insights that remain hidden in raw data. Yet this power comes with responsibility, as the choices made in creating visualizations can illuminate truth or obscure it and can guide understanding or mislead it. The act of visualization is fundamentally an act of translation, converting the precise but abstract language of data into the intuitive but subjective language of visual perception. This translation process involves countless decisions about what to show and what to hide, how to encode information in visual elements, and how to guide the viewer's attention and interpretation. Each of these decisions carries implications for how the underlying information will be understood and used. The human visual system, evolved to navigate physical environments and recognize patterns crucial for survival, brings both extraordinary capabilities and systematic limitations to the task of interpreting data visualizations. Understanding these capabilities and limitations is essential for creating visualizations that effectively communicate insights while avoiding the perceptual traps that can lead to misinterpretation. The democratization of data visualization tools has made it possible for anyone to create charts and graphs, but this accessibility has not automatically led to more effective communication. The ease of creating visualizations can mask the complexity of creating good visualizations, leading to a proliferation of charts that confuse rather than clarify, that overwhelm rather than inform, and that persuade through visual rhetoric rather than reveal through honest representation.

The Grammar of Graphics Principles of Effective Data Visualization

The foundation of effective data visualization rests on understanding the systematic relationships between data and visual elements, a framework that can be understood as a grammar of graphics. Just as linguistic grammar provides rules for combining words into meaningful sentences, visual grammar provides principles for combining graphical elements into meaningful representations of data. This grammar encompasses not only the technical aspects of encoding data in visual form but also the perceptual and cognitive principles that govern how humans interpret visual information. The idea of visual encoding lies at the heart of the grammar of graphics, describing how abstract data values are mapped to concrete visual properties such as position, length, area, color, and texture. These visual properties differ dramatically in their effectiveness for communicating different types of information. Position along a common scale represents the most accurate and efficient encoding for quantitative data, allowing viewers to make precise comparisons between values. Length and area encodings are less precise but can be effective for showing approximate relationships and proportions. Color encodings work well for categorical distinctions but can be misleading when applied to quantitative data without careful consideration of perceptual principles. The choice of visual encoding must be matched not only to the type of data being represented but also to the analytical task the visualization is intended to support. A visualization designed to enable precise comparisons between values requires different encoding choices than one intended to show overall trends or patterns. The grammar of graphics provides a framework for making these choices systematically rather than arbitrarily, ensuring that the visual design supports rather than undermines the intended analytical purpose. Scale and proportion play crucial roles in visual communication, yet they are among the most commonly mishandled aspects of data visualization. The human visual system is highly sensitive to proportional relationships, meaning that seemingly minor choices about axis ranges, aspect ratios, and scaling can dramatically alter the perception of patterns and trends. A time series chart that shows dramatic fluctuations when displayed with a narrow y-axis range might appear relatively stable when shown with a broader range that includes more context. Neither representation is inherently correct, but each tells a different story about the significance of the observed changes. The principle of proportional ink suggests that the amount of ink or visual space devoted to representing a data value should be proportional to the magnitude of that value. Violations of this principle, such as three-dimensional charts where volume grows faster than the underlying data values, can create misleading impressions about the relative importance of different data points. Similarly, the use of pictographic elements that scale inappropriately can exaggerate differences between values, leading viewers to draw incorrect conclusions about the underlying data. Color serves multiple functions in data visualization, from encoding quantitative and categorical information to directing attention and creating visual hierarchy. However, the effective use of color requires understanding both the perceptual properties of color and the cultural and contextual associations that colors carry. The human visual system perceives some color differences more readily than others, making certain color combinations more effective for distinguishing between categories or showing quantitative progressions. Sequential color schemes work well for showing ordered data such as temperatures or income levels, while diverging schemes are appropriate for data that has a meaningful center point, such as changes from a baseline or differences from an average. The accessibility of color choices represents both an ethical imperative and a practical necessity, as color blindness affects a significant portion of the population. Visualizations that rely solely on color distinctions to convey important information will be ineffective for these viewers, requiring designers to incorporate additional visual cues such as patterns, shapes, or labels to ensure universal accessibility.

Typography and text elements in data visualization serve not merely decorative purposes but functional ones, providing context, explanation, and guidance that help viewers interpret visual elements correctly. The hierarchy of text elements, from titles and subtitles to axis labels and annotations, creates a structure that guides the viewer through the visualization and provides the contextual information necessary for accurate interpretation. Poor typography choices can make even well-designed charts difficult to read and understand, while thoughtful typography can enhance comprehension and accessibility. The composition and layout of visualization elements determine how the viewer's attention flows through the display and which elements receive emphasis. The principles of visual design, borrowed from fields such as graphic design and art, provide guidance for creating compositions that are both aesthetically pleasing and functionally effective. The use of white space, alignment, and grouping helps organize information and reduce cognitive load, while techniques such as highlighting and annotation can direct attention to the most important insights. The chart junk, popularized by Edward Tufte, refers to visual elements that do not contribute to understanding the underlying data and may actually impede comprehension. Excessive decoration, unnecessary grid lines, redundant labels, and gratuitous three-dimensional effects can distract from the essential information and make charts harder to read. However, the complete elimination of all non-data elements can result in stark, difficult-to-interpret displays that lack the contextual cues necessary for understanding. The challenge lies in finding the appropriate balance between clarity and context, removing elements that genuinely impede understanding while retaining those that aid interpretation. Interactivity in data visualization opens new possibilities for exploration and understanding but also introduces new complexities in design and interpretation. Interactive elements such as filtering, zooming, and drill-down capabilities can allow viewers to explore data at multiple levels of detail and from different perspectives. However, poorly designed interactions can confuse users and lead to inconsistent interpretations, while the complexity of interactive visualizations can make them less accessible to some audiences. The temporal dimension of data presents particular challenges for visualization design, as patterns that occur over time may require different approaches than static cross-sectional data. Animation can be effective for showing how patterns evolve over time, but it can also make it difficult to compare values at different time points or to perceive overall trends. Static approaches such as small multiples or layered time series may be more effective for enabling the detailed comparisons that analytical tasks often require.

Storytelling with Data: Crafting Narratives that Resonate

Data storytelling transforms the abstract realm of numbers and statistics into compelling narratives that engage audiences, convey insights, and motivate action. This transformation requires more than simply presenting data in visual form; it demands the careful construction of narratives that guide audiences through a logical progression from initial curiosity to final understanding, weaving together quantitative evidence with qualitative context to create stories that resonate with human experience and motivation. The foundation of effective data storytelling lies in understanding that every dataset contains multiple potential stories, and the storyteller's role is to identify and craft the narrative that best serves the audience's needs and the analytical purpose. A single sales dataset might yield stories about seasonal trends, customer segmentation, product performance, competitive dynamics, or operational efficiency, depending on the questions being asked and the decisions that need to be made. The choice of which story to tell is not neutral; it reflects judgments about what is important, what is actionable, and what will resonate with the intended audience.

Narrative structure provides the organizing framework that transforms disconnected data points into coherent stories. The classical structure of setup, conflict, and resolution maps naturally onto many data stories, beginning with the establishment of context and expectations, proceeding through the identification of problems or opportunities revealed by the data, and concluding with insights and recommendations that resolve the initial tension. This structure helps audiences follow the logical flow of the analysis while maintaining engagement through the inherent drama of discovery and problem-solving. The narrative arc in data storytelling emphasizes the importance of pacing and progression in guiding audiences through complex information. Rather than overwhelming viewers with all available data at once, effective data stories reveal information gradually, building understanding step by step and creating moments of insight and revelation. This progressive disclosure allows audiences to absorb and process information at a manageable pace while maintaining the momentum necessary to sustain attention through lengthy presentations or complex analyses. Character development in data storytelling involves making abstract entities such as customer segments, market forces, or organizational units feel concrete and relatable to audiences. Rather than referring to "Segment A" or "Product Category 3," effective data stories develop these entities as characters with distinct personalities, motivations, and trajectories. A customer segment becomes "busy professionals seeking convenience," complete with specific behaviors, preferences, and pain points that audiences can understand and empathize with. This characterization makes the data more memorable and actionable by connecting it to human experiences and motivations. The role of conflict and tension in data storytelling cannot be underestimated, as these elements create the engagement and urgency that motivate audiences to pay attention and take action. Data stories without conflict or tension often fail to capture attention or inspire action, regardless of the quality of the underlying analysis. The conflict might be a performance gap that needs to be closed, a competitive threat that must be addressed, an opportunity that might be missed, or a mystery that demands explanation. The identification and articulation of this conflict provides the driving force that propels the narrative forward. Context serves as the foundation upon which data stories are built, providing the background information necessary for audiences to understand the significance of the patterns and relationships being presented. Without adequate context, even the most striking data visualizations may fail to convey their intended meaning or may be misinterpreted by audiences who lack the background knowledge to interpret them correctly. Effective context-setting involves not only providing factual background but also establishing the stakes and implications that make the data story relevant to the audience's concerns and objectives.

The use of analogies and metaphors in data storytelling helps make complex or abstract concepts accessible to audiences who may not have technical backgrounds or domain expertise. A well-chosen analogy can illuminate relationships and patterns that might otherwise remain opaque, while poorly chosen analogies can mislead or confuse. The key to effective analogical reasoning in data storytelling is selecting comparisons that capture the essential aspects of the phenomenon being described while avoiding misleading implications that might arise from pushing the analogy too far.

Emotional engagement represents a crucial but often overlooked dimension of data storytelling. While data analysis is often viewed as a purely rational endeavor, the reality is that audiences make decisions based on both rational evaluation and emotional response. Data stories that engage emotions as well as intellect are more likely to be remembered, understood, and acted upon. This emotional engagement can be achieved through various techniques, including the use of human examples and case studies, the highlighting of impacts on real people, and the creation of vivid imagery that helps audiences visualize the implications of the data. The pacing and rhythm of data stories significantly influence how well audiences can follow and retain the information being presented. Just as musical compositions use variation in tempo and dynamics to maintain interest and guide emotional response, effective data stories vary their pacing to create moments of intensity and reflection, building to climaxes and allowing for periods of consolidation. Dense, technical sections might be followed by simpler summary statements, while complex visualizations might be preceded by simpler introductory charts that prepare audiences for more sophisticated analysis. The credibility of data stories depends not only on the accuracy of the underlying analysis but also on the transparency and honesty with which limitations, uncertainties, and alternative interpretations are acknowledged. Audiences are often sophisticated enough to recognize when information is being selectively presented or when important caveats are being omitted, and the failure to acknowledge these limitations can undermine trust and credibility. Effective data storytellers build credibility by being forthright about what the data can and cannot tell us, acknowledging uncertainties and limitations while still drawing reasonable conclusions and recommendations. The adaptation of data stories to different audiences requires understanding not only what information is relevant to each group but also what communication styles, levels of detail, and types of evidence will be most persuasive. Technical audiences may appreciate detailed methodological discussions and comprehensive supporting evidence, while executive audiences may prefer high-level summaries focused on strategic implications. The same underlying analysis might be presented as a detailed technical report for data scientists, a summary dashboard for managers, and an infographic for general audiences, with each version tailored to its intended users while maintaining consistency in core messages and conclusions.

The iterative refinement of data stories through feedback and testing helps ensure that the intended messages are being effectively communicated and that audiences are drawing the intended conclusions. This refinement process might involve testing different versions of visualizations with focus groups, gathering feedback on draft presentations, or monitoring how audiences respond to and act on the information presented. The willingness to revise and improve data stories based on this feedback distinguishes effective communicators from those who assume that their initial instincts about effective communication are always correct.

Interactive Exploration: Engaging Audiences in the Discovery Process

Interactive data visualization transforms passive consumption of information into active exploration, enabling audiences to participate in the discovery process rather than simply receiving predetermined insights. This participatory approach can lead to deeper understanding, greater engagement, and more personalized insights, but it also introduces new challenges in design, usability, and interpretation that require careful consideration. The fundamental appeal of interactive exploration lies in its ability to accommodate the diverse interests, perspectives, and questions that different audience members bring to a dataset. Rather than forcing all viewers to follow the same predetermined path through the data, interactive visualizations allow each user to pursue their own lines of inquiry, drill down into areas of particular interest, and construct their own understanding of the patterns and relationships present in the data. This personalization can lead to insights that might never emerge from static presentations, as users discover unexpected connections and patterns that resonate with their unique knowledge and experience. The design of effective interactive visualizations requires balancing flexibility with guidance, providing enough freedom for meaningful exploration while offering sufficient structure to prevent users from becoming lost or overwhelmed. Too much flexibility can lead to confusion and ineffective use, while too little can make the interaction feel constrained and artificial. The challenge lies in creating what might be called "guided discovery," where users feel free to explore while being subtly directed toward the most important and actionable insights. Navigation and interface design play crucial roles in determining whether interactive visualizations enhance or impede understanding. Users must be able to quickly understand what actions are possible, how to perform those actions, and what the results of their actions mean. Poor interface design can create barriers that prevent users from accessing the insights contained in the data, while excellent interface design can make exploration feel natural and intuitive. The principles of user experience design, borrowed from software development and human-computer interaction, provide valuable guidance for creating interfaces that support rather than hinder analytical thinking. The progressive disclosure applies particularly well to interactive data visualization, where users can begin with high-level overviews and gradually drill down into more detailed information as their interest and understanding develop. This layered approach prevents cognitive overload while ensuring that detailed information is available when needed. Effective implementations of progressive disclosure provide clear visual cues about where additional detail is available and make it easy for users to move between different levels of granularity without losing their place or context. Real-time feedback and responsiveness are essential characteristics of effective interactive visualizations, as delays or unresponsive interfaces can break the flow of exploration and discovery.

Users expect immediate visual responses to their actions, whether they are filtering data, changing parameters, or exploring different views of the same information. Technical performance considerations, including data processing speed and rendering efficiency, become crucial factors in determining whether interactive visualizations achieve their intended purpose of facilitating exploration. The preservation of context during interactive exploration helps users maintain their orientation and understanding as they navigate through different views and subsets of the data. Users can easily become lost in complex datasets, losing track of how their current view relates to the overall picture or forgetting the path they took to reach their current location. Effective interactive visualizations provide contextual cues such as breadcrumb navigation, overview windows, or persistent reference information that help users maintain their bearings throughout the exploration process. Collaborative exploration capabilities extend the benefits of interactive visualization beyond individual users to teams and groups who need to work together to understand complex data. Features such as shared bookmarks, annotation capabilities, and discussion threads can transform individual exploration into collaborative knowledge building, where team members can share discoveries, build on each other's insights, and collectively develop understanding that no individual could achieve alone. However, the design of collaborative features requires careful consideration of workflow, permissions, and communication patterns to ensure that collaboration enhances rather than complicates the analytical process. The documentation and sharing of interactive discoveries present unique challenges, as the insights gained through exploration may be difficult to communicate to others who did not participate in the discovery process. Users may need tools for capturing and sharing their exploratory paths, creating snapshots of interesting configurations, or generating static summaries of their interactive findings. Without these capabilities, the insights gained through interactive exploration may remain isolated and fail to contribute to broader organizational understanding.

Personalization and customization features allow users to adapt interactive visualizations to their specific needs, preferences, and analytical workflows. This might include the ability to save custom views, create personalized dashboards, or modify the appearance and behavior of visualizations to match individual working styles. However, excessive customization options can overwhelm users and make it difficult to maintain consistency across different users and use cases. The challenge lies in identifying which customization options provide genuine value and which merely add complexity without corresponding benefits. The educational potential of interactive visualization extends beyond simply presenting information to actually teaching users about data analysis concepts and techniques. Well-designed interactive tools can help users develop intuitions about statistical relationships, understand the effects of different analytical choices, and learn to ask better questions of data. This educational dimension transforms interactive visualization from a presentation medium into a learning environment where users develop analytical skills alongside domain knowledge.

Quality control and validation become more complex in interactive environments where users can generate their own analyses and interpretations rather than simply consuming pre-validated insights. Interactive tools may need to incorporate safeguards against common analytical errors, provide warnings about potential misinterpretations, or offer guidance about appropriate and inappropriate conclusions. The balance between providing helpful guidance and maintaining user autonomy requires careful consideration of the target audience's analytical sophistication and the potential consequences of misinterpretation. The measurement and evaluation of interactive visualization effectiveness presents unique challenges, as traditional metrics such as accuracy of interpretation or speed of task completion may not capture the full value of exploratory discovery. Users may gain valuable insights that were not part of the original design intent, or they may develop understanding that is difficult to measure through conventional assessment methods. New evaluation approaches may need to focus on learning outcomes, engagement levels, and the quality of questions generated rather than simply the correctness of answers provided.

7

MACHINE LEARNING AND PATTERN RECOGNITION AUGMENTING HUMAN INTELLIGENCE

The intersection of human intelligence and machine learning represents one of the most profound developments in contemporary data analysis, creating new possibilities for discovery while simultaneously introducing new challenges for interpretation and application. Machine learning algorithms excel at processing vast amounts of data, identifying complex patterns, and making predictions with remarkable accuracy, yet they operate in ways that are often opaque to human understanding and may miss contextual nuances that human analysts would immediately recognize. The relationship between human and machine intelligence in data analysis is not simply one of replacement or competition, but rather one of complementary capabilities that can be combined to achieve insights neither could accomplish alone. Human analysts bring contextual understanding, domain expertise, creative problem-solving abilities, and the capacity to recognize when patterns make practical sense within the broader world. Machine learning systems contribute computational power, the ability to process information on a scale, freedom from cognitive biases, and the capacity to detect subtle patterns that might escape human attention. This partnership between human and artificial intelligence transforms the role of the data analyst from someone who manually searches for patterns to someone who guides, interprets, and contextualizes machine-discovered insights. The analyst becomes a translator between the mathematical world of algorithms and the practical world of business decisions, ensuring that machine learning outputs are properly understood, appropriately applied, and meaningfully integrated into human decision-making processes. The evolution of machine learning capabilities has democratized access to sophisticated analytical techniques, making it possible for organizations without extensive technical resources to apply advanced pattern recognition methods to their data. However, this democratization has also created new risks, as powerful analytical tools can be applied incorrectly by users who may not fully understand their assumptions, limitations, or appropriate use cases. The effective integration of machine learning into organizational decision-making requires not only technical competence but also a deep understanding of how these tools fit within broader analytical and strategic contexts.

Supervised Learning: Teaching Machines to Recognize Known Patterns

Supervised learning represents the most familiar and widely applicable branch of machine learning, encompassing methods that learn to make predictions or classifications based on examples of input-output relationships. The fundamental premise of supervised learning is that patterns observed in historical data can be used to make predictions about new, unseen cases, assuming that the underlying relationships remain stable over time and across different contexts. The process of supervised learning begins with the careful preparation and curation of training data, a task that requires deep understanding of both the domain being studied and the technical requirements of the chosen algorithms. The quality of the training data fundamentally determines the quality of the resulting models, yet data preparation often receives insufficient attention relative to its importance. Poor quality training data, whether due to measurement errors, sampling biases, or inadequate representation of the phenomenon being studied, will inevitably lead to poor model performance regardless of the sophistication of the algorithms employed.

The selection and engineering of features represents one of the most critical aspects of supervised learning, requiring analysts to identify which characteristics of the data are most relevant for the prediction task at hand. This process involves both technical considerations about how different types of information can be effectively encoded for machine learning algorithms and domain expertise about which relationships are likely to be meaningful and stable. Feature engineering often involves transforming raw data into derived variables that better capture the underlying patterns, such as calculating ratios, differences, or aggregations that highlight important relationships. The challenge of feature selection becomes particularly acute when dealing with high-dimensional datasets where the number of potential features far exceeds the number of training examples. In such situations, models may appear to perform well on training data while failing catastrophically on new data, a phenomenon known as overfitting. The curse of dimensionality affects not only model performance but also interpretability, as models with hundreds or thousands of features become essentially impossible for human analysts to understand or validate based on domain knowledge. Classification tasks, where the goal is to assign new examples to discrete categories, require careful consideration of how different types of errors impact downstream decisions. The confusion between different classes is rarely symmetric in its consequences; misclassifying a legitimate transaction as fraudulent may be annoying to a customer, while misclassifying a fraudulent transaction as legitimate may result in significant financial losses. The development of effective classification models requires understanding these asymmetric costs and adjusting the decision thresholds and model objectives accordingly. Regression tasks, focused on predicting continuous numerical outcomes, present their own unique challenges related to the interpretation and validation of predictions. Unlike classification tasks where accuracy can be measured simply by counting correct and incorrect predictions, regression models require more sophisticated evaluation metrics that account for the magnitude and distribution of prediction errors. The relationship between statistical significance and practical significance becomes particularly important in regression contexts, where models may identify relationships that are statistically reliable but too small to be actionable. The temporal dimension adds complexity to supervised learning when the goal is to make predictions about future events based on historical patterns. Time series prediction requires careful consideration of trends, seasonality, and structural breaks that may make historical relationships poor predictors of future outcomes. The challenge of concept drift, where the underlying relationships change over time, means that models must be continuously monitored and updated to maintain their predictive accuracy. Cross-validation and model evaluation techniques provide essential safeguards against overoptimistic assessments of model performance, but they must be implemented carefully to avoid subtle forms of data leakage that can make models appear more accurate than they actually are. The proper implementation of validation procedures requires understanding not only the technical aspects of splitting data into training and testing sets but also the temporal and logical relationships that determine which examples can legitimately be used to predict others. Ensemble methods, which combine predictions from multiple models to achieve better performance than any single model alone, illustrate the power of diversity in machine learning approaches. Random forests, gradient boosting, and other ensemble techniques work by exploiting the fact that different models tend to make different types of errors, and these errors can partially cancel out when predictions are combined appropriately. However, the interpretability of ensemble models presents significant challenges, as the logic behind their predictions becomes distributed across multiple models rather than concentrated in a single, comprehensible framework. The selection of appropriate algorithms for supervised learning tasks requires balancing multiple considerations, including predictive accuracy, computational efficiency, interpretability, and robustness to violations of underlying assumptions. Linear models offer interpretability and computational efficiency but may miss important nonlinear relationships. Tree-based methods can capture complex interactions but may be unstable and prone to overfitting. Neural networks can model highly complex patterns but operate as black boxes that provide little insight into their decision-making processes.

The evaluation of supervised learning models extends beyond simple accuracy metrics to encompass fairness, robustness, and generalizability considerations that are crucial for real-world applications. Models that perform well on average may exhibit systematic biases against certain subgroups, fail catastrophically on edge cases, or prove fragile when deployed in environments that differ from their training conditions. The responsible deployment of supervised learning requires comprehensive evaluation that considers these broader implications rather than focusing solely on aggregate performance metrics.

Unsupervised Discovery: Finding Hidden Structures in Data

Unsupervised learning represents perhaps the most intellectually fascinating branch of machine learning, encompassing methods that seek to discover hidden patterns, structures, and relationships in data without the guidance of predetermined target variables or outcome labels. Unlike supervised learning, where the goal is clearly defined by historical examples of desired outputs, unsupervised learning ventures into the realm of pure discovery, attempting to find meaningful organization in data that may initially appear chaotic or random. The fundamental challenge of unsupervised learning lies in defining what constitutes a meaningful pattern or structure in the absence of external validation criteria. Without clear success metrics, analysts must rely on a combination of algorithmic objectives, domain expertise, and subjective judgment to evaluate whether discovered patterns represent genuine insights or mere artifacts of the analytical process. This ambiguity makes unsupervised learning both more creative and more dangerous than supervised approaches, as the potential for self-deception and spurious discoveries is significantly higher. Cluster analysis represents one of the most widely applied forms of unsupervised learning, seeking to identify groups of similar observations within datasets. The appeal of clustering lies in its promise to reveal natural categories or segments that exist within data, providing organizational structures that can guide decision-making and strategic planning. However, the apparent simplicity of clustering masks significant complexity in determining appropriate similarity measures, choosing optimal numbers of clusters, and interpreting the meaning of discovered groupings. The choice of distance or similarity measures fundamentally shapes the types of clusters that algorithms can discover, yet this choice often receives insufficient attention from practitioners. Euclidean distance works well for numerical data where all variables have similar scales and importance, but it may be inappropriate when variables have different units, ranges, or meanings. Cosine similarity captures patterns based on proportional relationships rather than absolute magnitudes, making it suitable for high-dimensional data such as text or customer behavior profiles. More sophisticated similarity measures can incorporate domain knowledge about which types of differences are most meaningful for particular applications. The curse of dimensionality affects clustering algorithms particularly severely, as high-dimensional spaces tend to make all points appear equally distant from each other, making it difficult to identify meaningful groupings. This phenomenon requires careful preprocessing and dimensionality reduction techniques that preserve the most important patterns while eliminating noise and irrelevant variation. Principal component analysis, t-SNE, and other dimensionality reduction methods can help make clustering more effective, but they introduce their own assumptions and limitations that must be understood and validated. The interpretation of discovered clusters requires combining algorithmic output with domain expertise to determine whether identified groupings represent meaningful and actionable segments. Clusters that appear statistically significant may not correspond to practically important distinctions, while subtle but important differences may be obscured by more obvious but less relevant variations. The validation of cluster quality requires multiple approaches, including statistical measures of cluster coherence and separation, practical evaluation of whether clusters correspond to known categories, and assessment of whether cluster-based strategies lead to improved outcomes. Association rule mining seeks to identify relationships between different variables or events, discovering patterns such as "customers who purchase product A are also likely to purchase product B" or "server errors of type X are often followed by errors of type Y." The ubiquity of association rule mining in applications such as market basket analysis and recommendation systems has made it one of the most commercially successful unsupervised learning techniques, yet its apparent simplicity can mask significant challenges in interpretation and application. The measurement of association strength requires careful consideration of base rates and statistical significance to avoid identifying spurious relationships that appear strong but are actually due to chance or confounding factors. Metrics such as support, confidence, and lift provide different perspectives on the strength and reliability of discovered associations, but none alone is sufficient for determining whether a relationship is meaningful and actionable. The evaluation of association rules must also consider practical factors such as the cost and feasibility of acting on discovered relationships. Anomaly detection represents another important application of unsupervised learning, seeking to identify observations that deviate significantly from normal patterns. The challenge of anomaly detection lies in distinguishing between genuinely unusual events that warrant attention and natural variation that falls within the expected range of normal behavior. This distinction requires understanding not only the statistical properties of the data but also the practical implications of different types of anomalies.

The definition of "normal" behavior in anomaly detection depends heavily on the temporal and contextual factors that influence the phenomenon being studied. Patterns that appear anomalous when viewed in isolation may be perfectly normal when considered within their proper context, while genuinely unusual events may be masked by seasonal variations or other predictable fluctuations. Effective anomaly detection requires sophisticated modeling approaches that can capture the complex, multi-dimensional nature of normal behavior while remaining sensitive to truly unusual events. Dimensionality reduction techniques such as principal component analysis, independent component analysis, and manifold learning methods serve both as preprocessing steps for other analyses and as analytical techniques in their own right. These methods seek to identify lower-dimensional representations of high-dimensional data that preserve the most important patterns while eliminating noise and redundancy. The challenge lies in determining how much dimensionality reduction is appropriate and ensuring that the reduced representation captures the aspects of the data that are most relevant for downstream analyses. The interpretability of dimensionality reduction results requires careful attention to what the reduced dimensions represent and how they relate to the original variables. Principal components may be difficult to interpret when they represent complex combinations of many original variables, while methods that produce more interpretable dimensions may sacrifice some accuracy in data representation. The trade-off between interpretability and accuracy must be evaluated based on the intended use of the dimensionality reduction results. Market segmentation represents one of the most important commercial applications of unsupervised learning, combining clustering, dimensionality reduction, and domain expertise to identify distinct customer groups with different needs, preferences, and behaviors. Effective market segmentation requires not only statistical analysis of customer data but also a deep understanding of market dynamics, competitive positioning, and operational capabilities that determine which segments can be effectively targeted. The validation of market segmentation results requires demonstrating that identified segments exhibit meaningful differences in outcomes such as purchase behavior, response to marketing campaigns, or lifetime value. Segments that appear distinct in demographic or behavioral characteristics may not translate into actionable business opportunities if they do not respond differently to available interventions or if the cost of targeting them exceeds their potential value.

The Human-AI Partnership: Combining Algorithmic Power with Human Intuition

The effective integration of machine learning capabilities with human expertise represents one of the most significant opportunities and challenges in contemporary data analysis. This partnership requires understanding not only the technical capabilities and limitations of algorithms but also the cognitive strengths and biases of human decision-makers, creating collaborative frameworks that leverage the best of both while mitigating their respective weaknesses. Human intuition and domain expertise provide crucial capabilities that complement algorithmic analysis in several key areas. Humans excel at recognizing when patterns make sense within broader contextual frameworks, identifying when algorithmic outputs violate fundamental principles or known constraints, and adapting analytical approaches when underlying conditions change in ways that algorithms cannot detect. Human analysts can also provide the creative problem-solving and hypothesis generation that often drive the most valuable analytical insights, while algorithms excel at testing and refining these hypotheses systematically. The human-in-the-loop machine learning recognizes that many analytical tasks benefit from continuous interaction between human expertise and algorithmic processing rather than treating them as separate, sequential phases. Interactive machine learning systems allow human experts to guide algorithmic discovery by providing feedback, adjusting parameters, and incorporating domain knowledge throughout the analytical process. This collaborative approach can lead to insights that neither humans nor algorithms could achieve independently while ensuring that analytical output remain grounded in practical understanding. Active learning represents one important manifestation of human-AI collaboration, where algorithms identify the most informative examples for human review and labeling. Rather than requiring humans to label large amounts of training data randomly, active learning focuses human effort on the cases where expert judgment can most improve model performance. This approach not only reduces the human effort required for model development but also ensures that human expertise is applied where it can have the greatest impact on algorithmic accuracy.

The interpretability of machine learning models becomes crucial for effective human-AI collaboration, as humans cannot provide meaningful guidance or validation for algorithms whose decision-making processes they cannot understand. Explainable AI techniques seek to make algorithmic reasoning more transparent and comprehensible, providing insights into which factors drive predictions and how different inputs influence outputs. However, the goal of interpretability must be balanced against model accuracy, as the most interpretable models are often not the most accurate, and vice versa. The development of effective explanations for machine learning models requires understanding not only the technical aspects of how algorithms work but also the cognitive needs and limitations of the humans who will use these explanations. Different stakeholders may need different types of explanations, from technical details about feature importance for data scientists to high-level summaries of decision logic for business executives. The effectiveness of explanations depends not only on their technical accuracy but also on their ability to support human decision-making and build appropriate trust in algorithmic outputs. Trust calibration represents a critical challenge in human-AI partnerships, as both over-reliance on algorithmic outputs and excessive skepticism can lead to poor decisions. Humans must develop accurate mental models of when algorithms are likely to be reliable and when they are likely to fail, adjusting their reliance accordingly. This calibration requires not only understanding algorithmic capabilities and limitations in general but also developing intuitions about how these capabilities apply to specific contexts and use cases. The phenomenon of algorithm aversion, where humans systematically under-rely on algorithmic advice even when it is more accurate than human judgment, presents significant challenges for realizing the benefits of human-AI collaboration. This aversion may stem from a variety of factors, including a lack of understanding about how algorithms work, a loss of control over decision-making processes, or cultural biases that favor human over machine judgment. Overcoming algorithm aversion requires not only technical improvements in algorithmic performance and interpretability but also organizational and cultural changes that support appropriate trust in automated systems.

Conversely, automation bias, where humans over-rely on algorithmic outputs without sufficient critical evaluation, can lead to the acceptance of flawed or inappropriate recommendations. The sophistication and apparent objectivity of machine learning systems can create false confidence in their outputs, leading humans to abdicate their responsibility for critical thinking and validation. Effective human-AI collaboration requires maintaining healthy skepticism and validation practices even when working with highly sophisticated algorithms. The design of human-AI interfaces plays a crucial role in determining how effectively humans and algorithms can collaborate. Interfaces that present algorithmic outputs without context or uncertainty information may encourage inappropriate reliance, while interfaces that provide too much technical detail may overwhelm non-expert users. Effective interface design must balance transparency with usability, providing enough information for appropriate trust calibration without creating cognitive overload. Workflow integration represents another critical factor in successful human-AI collaboration, as algorithmic capabilities must be embedded within existing organizational processes and decision-making frameworks. This integration requires understanding not only the technical requirements for deploying machine learning systems but also the human factors that determine how these systems will be used in practice. The most sophisticated algorithms will provide little value if they cannot be effectively integrated into the workflows and decision processes of their intended users. The continuous learning and improvement of human-AI partnerships requires systematic approaches to monitoring performance, gathering feedback, and refining both algorithmic and human components of collaborative systems. This improvement process must account for the dynamic nature of both human expertise and algorithmic capabilities, as both evolve over time through experience and training. Organizations must develop capabilities for managing this evolution and ensuring that human-AI partnerships continue to deliver value as conditions change. The ethical implications of human-AI collaboration extend beyond the technical performance of algorithms to encompass questions of responsibility, accountability, and fairness in decision-making processes. When humans and algorithms collaborate in making decisions that affect other people, it becomes crucial to maintain clear accountability structures and ensure that the benefits and risks of these decisions are distributed fairly. The complexity of human-AI partnerships can make it difficult to assign responsibility for outcomes, creating challenges for governance and oversight.

The training and development of human capabilities to work effectively with AI systems represents an ongoing organizational challenge that extends beyond technical training to encompass cognitive skills, decision-making frameworks, and collaborative practices. Humans must learn not only how to use algorithmic tools effectively but also how to maintain their own analytical capabilities and judgment in an increasingly automated environment. This training must be ongoing rather than one-time, as both human capabilities and AI systems continue to evolve rapidly. The measurement and evaluation of human-AI collaboration effectiveness requires metrics that go beyond simple accuracy or efficiency measures to encompass the quality of the collaborative process itself. Traditional performance metrics may not capture the value of improved decision-making processes, enhanced learning and discovery, or better risk management that can result from effective human-AI partnerships. Organizations must develop new approaches to measuring and optimizing collaborative performance that account for both human and algorithmic contributions to overall outcomes.

8

EXPERIMENTAL DESIGN AND CAUSAL INFERENCE BEYOND CORRELATION

The relationship between correlation and causation represents one of the most fundamental challenges in scientific inquiry and data analysis. While statistical associations can reveal patterns and relationships within data, they cannot, by themselves, establish the directional flow of influence that defines true causality. This distinction becomes critical when moving from descriptive analysis to prescriptive action, from understanding what happened to determining what interventions might produce desired outcomes. The challenge of causal inference extends far beyond academic curiosity. In medicine, the difference between correlation and causation can mean the difference between effective treatment and harmful intervention. In economics, it determines whether policy recommendations will achieve their intended effects or create unintended consequences. In technology, it influences whether algorithmic decisions reflect genuine predictive relationships or spurious correlations that fail when deployed in real-world contexts.

Consider the classic example of ice cream sales and drowning incidents, which show a strong positive correlation during summer months. A naive interpretation might suggest that ice cream consumption somehow causes drowning, leading to misguided policies restricting ice cream sales near beaches. The true causal structure involves temperature as a common cause, influencing both ice cream purchases and swimming activity, with the latter affecting drowning risk. This simple example illustrates why establishing causality requires more than observing statistical relationships. The confounding variable problem extends to virtually every domain of observational research. In educational studies, students who receive tutoring often show improved test scores, but this correlation doesn't necessarily imply that tutoring causes improvement. Students who receive tutoring may come from families with higher socioeconomic status, greater educational emphasis, or other characteristics that independently influence academic performance. Without accounting for these confounding factors, conclusions about tutoring effectiveness remain uncertain. The challenge becomes even more complex when dealing with dynamic systems where variables influence each other over time. Economic indicators provide a compelling example. Employment levels and consumer spending show strong correlation, but the causal relationship flows in both directions. Higher employment leads to increased spending power, which drives demand for goods and services, which in turn creates more employment opportunities. This feedback loop makes it difficult to identify primary causal drivers using observational data alone.

The Gold Standard: Randomized Controlled Experiments

Randomized controlled experiments represent the most powerful method for establishing causal relationships because they address the fundamental problem of confounding through random assignment. When participants or units are randomly assigned to treatment and control groups, the randomization process ensures that both observed and unobserved characteristics are distributed similarly across groups. This creates conditions where any systematic differences in outcomes can be attributed to the treatment intervention rather than pre-existing differences between groups. The power of randomization lies in its ability to handle unknown confounders. While researchers can control measured variables through statistical techniques, they cannot account for unmeasured factors that might influence both treatment assignment and outcomes. Randomization addresses this limitation by making treatment assignment independent of all participant characteristics, measured or unmeasured. This independence forms the foundation for causal inference in experimental settings. The design of randomized experiments requires careful attention to multiple components. Sample size calculations must ensure sufficient statistical power to detect meaningful effects while accounting for expected variability in outcomes. The randomization process itself must be truly random and properly implemented to avoid systematic biases. Blinding procedures, where possible, prevent participants and researchers from knowing treatment assignments, reducing the risk of placebo effects and experimenter bias. Control group selection presents another critical design consideration. In medical trials, placebo controls help isolate the specific effects of active treatments from general effects of receiving attention or intervention. In social science experiments, the choice of control condition determines which causal questions can be answered. A study comparing a new teaching method to traditional instruction answers different questions than one comparing the same method to no instruction at all. The measurement of outcomes must align with the research questions and theoretical frameworks guiding the study. Primary outcomes should be specified before data collection begins to avoid the temptation to selectively report favorable results. Multiple outcome measures can provide a more comprehensive understanding of treatment effects, but they also increase the risk of false discoveries due to multiple testing. Pre-registration of analysis plans has become increasingly important for maintaining the integrity of experimental research. Randomized experiments also require careful attention to external validity, the extent to which findings generalize beyond the specific experimental context. Laboratory experiments offer high internal validity through tight control over conditions but may sacrifice external validity if laboratory conditions differ substantially from real-world settings. Field experiments conducted in natural environments often provide better external validity but may face challenges in maintaining experimental control.

The timeline for observing effects presents another important consideration. Some interventions produce immediate effects that can be measured shortly after implementation, while others require extended observation periods to capture their full impact. Educational interventions, for example, may show immediate effects on test scores but require longer follow-up to assess impacts on educational attainment or career outcomes. The choice of measurement timing affects both the practical feasibility of experiments and the types of causal claims that can be supported. Compliance with treatment assignment represents a common challenge in experimental research. Participants assigned to treatment groups may not fully comply with the intervention protocol, while those in control groups may seek out similar treatments elsewhere. Intention-to-treat analysis preserves the benefits of randomization by analyzing participants according to their original group assignments, but it may underestimate treatment effects when compliance is imperfect. Instrumental variable approaches can help estimate the effects of actually receiving treatment rather than being assigned to treatment.

Natural Experiments: Finding Causation in Observational Data

When controlled experiments are impractical, unethical, or impossible, natural experiments provide alternative approaches for causal inference. Natural experiments occur when external forces create variation in treatment assignment that mimics the random assignment of controlled experiments. These quasi-experimental designs leverage naturally occurring variations to identify causal effects from observational data. Regression discontinuity designs represent one powerful class of natural experiments. These designs exploit arbitrary cutoff points in assignment rules to create treatment and control groups that are similar in all respects except for treatment status. Educational research provides numerous examples, such as studies examining the effects of class size reduction by comparing students just above and below enrollment thresholds that trigger additional classroom assignments. The assumption underlying these designs is that students just above and below the threshold are essentially identical except for the treatment they receive. The validity of regression discontinuity designs depends critically on the assumption that assignment to treatment is based solely on crossing the specified threshold. If other factors change discontinuously at the same cutoff point, the design cannot isolate the treatment effect. Researchers must carefully examine whether policies, practices, or other interventions change at the threshold that might confound the estimated treatment effects. Instrumental variable approaches provide another strategy for causal inference in observational settings. An instrumental variable must satisfy three conditions: it must be correlated with the treatment variable of interest, it must affect the outcome only through its effect on treatment, and it must be uncorrelated with unobserved factors that influence the outcome. When these conditions are met, instrumental variables can identify causal effects even in the presence of unmeasured confounding. Geographic variation often provides compelling instrumental variables. Studies of education spending effects have used court-ordered school finance reforms as instruments, arguing that these reforms create exogenous variation in spending levels that is uncorrelated with other factors affecting student achievement. Similarly, research on the effects of military service has used draft lottery numbers as instruments, since lottery assignment was random and affected life outcomes primarily through military service. Weather patterns and natural disasters provide another source of instrumental variation. Agricultural studies have used rainfall variation to identify the effects of income on various outcomes, arguing that weather affects income through agricultural productivity but doesn't directly influence other outcome variables. Similarly, research on the effects of economic conditions has used earthquake timing as an instrument, since the timing of natural disasters is random but affects economic outcomes through destruction of capital and infrastructure. Difference-in-differences designs compare changes over time between treatment and control groups, relying on the assumption that both groups would have followed similar trends in the absence of treatment. These designs are particularly useful for evaluating policy interventions that affect some geographic areas or population groups but not others. The key identifying assumption is that the treatment and control groups would have experienced parallel trends in outcomes if the intervention had not occurred.

The parallel trends assumption cannot be directly tested since it involves counterfactual outcomes that are never observed. However, researchers can examine pre-treatment trends to assess whether treatment and control groups were following similar trajectories before the intervention. Significant differences in pre-treatment trends may indicate violations of the parallel trends assumption and threaten the validity of causal inferences. Matching methods attempt to create treatment and control groups that are similar on observed characteristics by pairing treated and untreated units with similar covariate values. Propensity score matching estimates the probability that each unit receives treatment based on observed characteristics and then matches units with similar propensity scores. The effectiveness of matching depends on having rich data on confounding variables and on the assumption that all important confounders are observed and measured. Synthetic control methods extend the matching approach by creating weighted combinations of control units that closely approximate the pre-treatment characteristics and outcomes of treated units. This approach is particularly useful when few control units are available or when no single control unit provides a good match for the treated unit. The method constructs a synthetic control unit that serves as a counterfactual for what would have happened to the treated unit without intervention.

The Hierarchy of Evidence: From Anecdote to Scientific Certainty

The strength of causal evidence varies dramatically across different research designs and methodological approaches. Understanding this hierarchy helps researchers choose appropriate methods for their questions and helps consumers of research evaluate the reliability of causal claims. The hierarchy reflects the degree to which different approaches can rule out alternative explanations for observed relationships. At the bottom of the evidence hierarchy lie anecdotal reports and case studies. While these sources can provide valuable insights and generate hypotheses, they offer little basis for causal inference. Individual cases cannot control confounding factors or establish that observed relationships generalize beyond specific circumstances. However, case studies play important roles in identifying new phenomena, exploring mechanisms, and providing detailed descriptions of complex processes. Cross-sectional observational studies occupy the next level of the hierarchy. These studies examine relationships between variables at a single point in time across different individuals or units. While cross-sectional studies can identify associations and patterns, they cannot establish temporal ordering between causes and effects. The inability to determine which variable changes first severely limits causal inference from cross-sectional data. Longitudinal observational studies strengthen causal inference by establishing temporal ordering between potential causes and effects. Following the same individuals or units over time allows researchers to observe whether changes in presumed causes precede changes in outcomes. However, longitudinal studies still face challenges from unmeasured confounding variables that might influence both causes and effects over time. Cohort studies represent a specific type of longitudinal design that follows groups of individuals who share common characteristics or experiences. These studies are particularly valuable for examining the long-term effects of exposures or interventions that cannot be randomly assigned for ethical reasons. Medical research has relied heavily on cohort studies to understand the health effects of behaviors like smoking, since randomly assigning people to smoke would be unethical. Case-control studies compare individuals who experienced particular outcomes with similar individuals who did not experience those outcomes, looking backward to identify potential causes. While case-control studies can be conducted more quickly and cheaply than cohort studies, they are susceptible to recall bias and other forms of systematic error. The retrospective nature of these studies makes it difficult to establish clear temporal relationships between causes and effects. Natural experiments occupy a higher position in the evidence hierarchy because they approximate the conditions of randomized experiments without requiring researchers to control treatment assignment. The strength of causal inference from natural experiments depends on how closely the natural assignment process approximates random assignment. The most convincing natural experiments involve assignment mechanisms that are as good as random, such as lottery systems or arbitrary administrative cutoffs.

Randomized controlled trials represent the gold standard for causal inference because random assignment eliminates systematic differences between treatment and control groups. The strength of evidence from randomized trials depends on factors such as sample size, the quality of randomization, adherence to treatment protocols, and the appropriateness of outcome measures. Well-designed and properly conducted randomized trials provide the strongest possible evidence for causal relationships. Meta-analyses and systematic reviews synthesize evidence across multiple studies to provide more comprehensive and reliable estimates of causal effects. These approaches can increase statistical power by combining results from smaller studies and can assess the consistency of findings across different contexts and populations. However, the quality of meta-analyses depends critically on the quality of the underlying studies and the appropriateness of combining results across different study designs and populations. The hierarchy of evidence provides a useful framework for evaluating research, but it should not be applied mechanically. The appropriate research design depends on the specific research question, ethical considerations, practical constraints, and the current state of knowledge in the field. Sometimes lower levels of evidence are more appropriate for particular questions or circumstances. Exploratory research might appropriately rely on case studies or cross-sectional analyses, while policy decisions might require the strongest possible evidence from randomized trials. The accumulation of evidence across multiple studies using different methods often provides more convincing support for causal relationships than any single study alone. Triangulation across different research designs can help address the limitations inherent in each approach. When observational studies, natural experiments, and randomized trials all point to similar conclusions, confidence in causal relationships increases substantially. The interpretation of evidence also depends on biological or theoretical plausibility. Causal claims that align with well-established theoretical frameworks or biological mechanisms may require less stringent evidence than claims that contradict existing knowledge. However, researchers must balance theoretical plausibility against empirical evidence, remaining open to findings that challenge existing paradigms while maintaining appropriate skepticism about extraordinary claims. The translation of research evidence into policy and practice requires careful consideration of external validity and implementation challenges. Evidence from highly controlled settings may not generalize to real-world conditions where implementation is imperfect and contexts vary. The strongest evidence for causal relationships in research settings may not translate directly into effective interventions in practice without additional adaptation and evaluation.

Understanding the hierarchy of evidence empowers researchers to design studies that provide the strongest possible evidence for their specific questions while recognizing the limitations inherent in different approaches. It also helps consumers of research evaluate the reliability of causal claims and make informed decisions about which findings warrant changes in policy or practice. The goal is not to dismiss lower levels of evidence but to interpret all evidence appropriately within its methodological context.

9

TIME SERIES AND DYNAMIC SYSTEMS UNDERSTANDING CHANGE OVER TIME

Time represents one of the most fundamental dimensions of human experience and scientific understanding, yet it poses unique challenges for data analysis and interpretation. Unlike cross-sectional data that captures snapshots of phenomena at single moments, time series data reveals the dynamic processes that govern how systems evolve, adapt, and respond to various influences over extended periods. This temporal dimension adds layers of complexity that require specialized analytical approaches and theoretical frameworks to understand properly. The analysis of temporal data differs fundamentally from static data analysis because observations are no longer independent. Each data point exists within a context defined by preceding observations, creating dependencies that must be acknowledged and modeled appropriately. These temporal dependencies often contain valuable information about underlying processes, but they also violate the independence assumptions underlying many statistical methods designed for cross-sectional data. Consider the challenge of understanding economic growth patterns. A country's gross domestic product in any given year depends heavily on its GDP in previous years, creating strong autocorrelation in the time series.

This dependency reflects real economic processes such as capital accumulation, technological advancement, and institutional development that evolve gradually over time. Ignoring these temporal relationships would miss crucial dynamics that govern economic development. The temporal structure of data also introduces questions about stationarity, the statistical property that describes whether the fundamental characteristics of a time series remain constant over time. Stationary time series have constant means, variances, and correlation structures, making them amenable to standard statistical analysis. Non-stationary series, by contrast, exhibit changing statistical properties that require different analytical approaches and often more sophisticated modeling techniques. Many real-world time series exhibit non-stationary behavior. Population growth typically follows exponential or logistic patterns rather than remaining constant over time. Technology adoption curves show characteristic S-shaped patterns as innovations diffuse through populations. Financial markets experience periods of high and low volatility that cluster together over time. These patterns reflect underlying dynamic processes that standard statistical methods may fail to capture adequately. The frequency and timing of observations also affect temporal analysis in important ways. High-frequency data, such as stock prices recorded every second or minute, may exhibit patterns and dependencies that are invisible in daily or monthly data. Seasonal patterns that are prominent in monthly data may be obscured when data are aggregated to annual frequencies. The choice of temporal resolution affects both the patterns that can be detected and the types of questions that can be addressed through analysis.

Temporal Patterns: Trends, Cycles, and Seasonal Variations

The decomposition of time series into component patterns represents one of the most fundamental approaches to temporal analysis. Most time series can be understood as combinations of trend, seasonal, cyclical, and irregular components, each reflecting different types of underlying processes. Understanding these components separately allows analysts to focus on specific aspects of temporal variation and to develop more accurate models and forecasts. Trends represent long-term directional changes in the time series that persist over extended periods. Population growth, technological progress, and climate change all produce trend components in relevant time series. Trends can be linear, exponential, logarithmic, or follow more complex functional forms depending on the underlying processes. Identifying and modeling trends accurately is crucial for understanding long-term dynamics and making projections about future states. Linear trends appear in many social and economic time series, particularly over shorter time periods where more complex dynamics may not be apparent. Educational attainment levels, urbanization rates, and life expectancy often exhibit approximately linear trends over periods of several decades. However, linear extrapolation can be misleading when underlying processes are inherently non-linear or when structural changes alter trend patterns. Exponential trends characterize many growth processes, particularly in their early stages. Population growth, technology adoption, and economic development often follow exponential patterns when constraints are minimal and growth compounds over time. Moore's law in computing represents a famous example of exponential technological progress that persisted for several decades. However, exponential growth is typically unsustainable in the long term due to resource constraints or saturation effects. Logistic trends combine initial exponential growth with eventual saturation as systems approach carrying capacity limits. These S-shaped curves appear frequently in diffusion processes, market penetration patterns, and biological systems. Internet adoption rates, smartphone penetration, and renewable energy deployment often follow logistic patterns as they spread through populations and eventually approach saturation levels.

Seasonal patterns reflect regular variations that repeat over fixed time periods, typically corresponding to natural cycles such as annual seasons, monthly patterns, or weekly rhythms. These patterns arise from various sources, including weather variations, institutional practices, cultural traditions, and biological rhythms. Understanding seasonal patterns is essential for many applications, from retail inventory management to energy demand forecasting.

Annual seasonality appears in numerous economic and social time series. Retail sales peak during holiday seasons, agricultural production follows planting and harvest cycles, and energy consumption varies with heating and cooling demands. These patterns are often predictable and stable over time, making them relatively straightforward to model and account for in analysis and forecasting. Weekly seasonality reflects human activity patterns and institutional schedules. Stock market volatility differs between weekdays and weekends, traffic patterns vary between weekdays and weekends, and social media activity shows distinct weekly rhythms. These patterns reflect the social organization of human activities and can be remarkably consistent across different contexts and time periods. Daily and hourly patterns reflect more detailed rhythms of human activity and natural processes. Electricity demand follows predictable daily patterns with peaks during evening hours and lows during overnight periods. Internet traffic, transportation usage, and communication patterns all exhibit characteristic daily rhythms that reflect human behavior patterns and biological circadian cycles. Cyclical patterns represent longer-term oscillations that do not have fixed periods like seasonal patterns. Business cycles in economics typically last several years but vary in duration and amplitude across different cycles. Climate oscillations such as El Niño and La Niña patterns affect weather and environmental conditions over multi-year periods but do not follow perfectly regular schedules. The distinction between cyclical and seasonal patterns is important for modeling and interpretation. Seasonal patterns have regular, predictable timing that makes them relatively easy to model and remove from time series. Cyclical patterns have variable timing and amplitude that make them more challenging to predict and model accurately. Economic recessions, for example, are cyclical phenomena that occur irregularly and with varying severity. Irregular or random components represent the unpredictable variations that remain after trend, seasonal, and cyclical components are removed. These components reflect the influence of random shocks, measurement errors, and other unpredictable factors that affect time series. While irregular components cannot be predicted individually, their statistical properties can often be modeled and incorporated into forecasting procedures. The relative importance of different components varies across time series and applications. Some series are dominated by trend components, making long-term forecasting relatively straightforward. Others are dominated by seasonal patterns, requiring careful attention to periodic variations. Still others are dominated by irregular components, making prediction more challenging and uncertain. Decomposition techniques help separate these components and understand their individual contributions to overall time series variation. Classical decomposition assumes that components combine additively, while other approaches allow for multiplicative or more complex interactions between components. The choice of decomposition method affects both the understanding of underlying processes and the accuracy of forecasts based on component models.

Forecasting: Predicting Future States from Historical Data

The prediction of future values from historical time series data represents one of the most important and challenging applications of temporal analysis. Forecasting combines statistical modeling with understanding of underlying processes to project likely future outcomes. The accuracy and reliability of forecasts depend on the stability of underlying patterns, the quality of historical data, and the appropriateness of modeling approaches for specific applications. Forecasting horizons vary dramatically depending on the application and the nature of underlying processes. Weather forecasting typically focuses on horizons from hours to weeks, reflecting the chaotic nature of atmospheric systems that limits predictability beyond certain time scales. Economic forecasting may extend to quarters or years, though accuracy generally decreases as forecasting horizons increase. Population projections may extend decades into the future for planning purposes, though they are subject to considerable uncertainty. The choice of forecasting method depends on various factors, including the characteristics of the time series, the forecasting horizon, the accuracy requirements, and the availability of explanatory variables. Simple methods such as moving averages or exponential smoothing may be appropriate for some applications, while complex econometric models or machine learning approaches may be necessary for others. Moving averages represent one of the simplest forecasting approaches, predicting future values as averages of recent historical observations. Simple moving averages give equal weight to all observations within the averaging window, while weighted moving averages allow different weights for different observations. These methods work well for time series with relatively stable patterns and minimal trend or seasonal components.

Exponential smoothing extends the moving average concept by giving exponentially decreasing weights to older observations. This approach automatically adapts to changes in time series patterns while maintaining computational simplicity. Various extensions of exponential smoothing can handle trend and seasonal components, making these methods applicable to a wide range of time series.

The Holt-Winters method extends exponential smoothing to handle both trend and seasonal components simultaneously. This approach uses separate smoothing parameters for level, trend, and seasonal components, allowing the method to adapt to changes in each component over time.

The method can handle both additive and multiplicative seasonal patterns and has proven effective for many business and economic forecasting applications. Autoregressive models predict future values based on linear combinations of past values, capturing the temporal dependencies that characterize many time series. The order of an autoregressive model determines how many past values are used in the prediction equation. Model selection involves balancing the explanatory power of including more past values against the increased complexity and potential overfitting risks. Moving average models predict future values based on linear combinations of past forecast errors rather than past observed values. These models capture the effects of random shocks that influence time series over multiple periods. Combined autoregressive moving average models incorporate both types of dependencies and provide flexible frameworks for modeling complex temporal patterns. Seasonal autoregressive integrated moving average models extend the basic ARIMA framework to handle seasonal patterns explicitly. These models include both non-seasonal and seasonal autoregressive and moving average components, allowing them to capture complex temporal dependencies at multiple time scales. Model identification and estimation require careful analysis of time series characteristics and extensive diagnostic checking.

Vector autoregression models extend univariate autoregressive models to multiple time series, allowing for interactions and feedback effects between different variables. These models are particularly useful for economic and financial forecasting where variables influence each other over time. For example, interest rates, inflation, and unemployment rates are interconnected in ways that univariate models cannot capture adequately. Regression-based forecasting approaches incorporate explanatory variables along with temporal patterns to improve forecast accuracy. These methods are particularly useful when leading indicators or causal variables are available to help predict future outcomes. Economic forecasting often relies on regression models that include variables such as interest rates, government spending, and consumer confidence as predictors. Machine learning approaches to forecasting have gained popularity as computational power has increased and new algorithms have been developed. Neural networks, support vector machines, and ensemble methods can capture complex non-linear relationships and interactions that traditional statistical methods might miss. However, these approaches often require large amounts of data and may be difficult to interpret or explain. Cross-validation techniques help evaluate forecasting performance and select appropriate models from among competing alternatives. Time series cross-validation differs from standard cross-validation because temporal ordering must be preserved. Rolling window approaches train models on historical data and evaluate performance on subsequent periods, simulating realistic forecasting scenarios. Forecast accuracy measures provide quantitative assessments of forecasting performance using metrics such as mean absolute error, root mean squared error and mean absolute percentage error. Different accuracy measures may favor different types of forecasts, so the choice of evaluation criteria should align with the specific objectives and constraints of the forecasting application. Forecast intervals provide measures of uncertainty around point forecasts, acknowledging that future outcomes are inherently uncertain. These intervals help decision-makers understand the reliability of forecasts and make appropriate allowances for uncertainty in planning and decision-making. The construction of forecast intervals requires assumptions about the distribution of forecast errors that may not always be satisfied in practice. Combining forecasts with multiple methods often produces more accurate and robust predictions than relying on any single approach. Forecast combination can be as simple as averaging predictions from different models or as sophisticated as using weighted combinations that adapt to changing relative performance. The principle behind forecast combination is that different methods may capture different aspects of underlying patterns and combining them can reduce overall forecast error.

Complex Systems: How Small Changes Create Large Effects

The study of complex systems reveals how simple rules, and small perturbations, can generate dramatically different outcomes over time. These systems exhibit behaviors that cannot be understood by analyzing individual components in isolation but emerge from the interactions and feedback loops between system elements. Understanding complex systems is crucial for interpreting time series data from social, economic, biological, and physical systems that exhibit non-linear dynamics. Chaos theory provides a framework for understanding how deterministic systems can produce apparently random behavior. Chaotic systems are characterized by sensitive dependence on initial conditions, meaning that tiny differences in starting points can lead to vastly different trajectories over time. This sensitivity limits the predictability of chaotic systems even when the underlying rules are completely known and deterministic. The logistic map provides a simple example of how complex dynamics can emerge from simple rules. This mathematical model describes population growth with environmental constraints and exhibits a remarkable range of behaviors depending on parameter values. For some parameter ranges, the system reaches stable equilibrium. For others, it oscillates between different values or exhibits completely chaotic behavior with no apparent pattern. Weather systems exemplify chaotic dynamics in natural phenomena. Small differences in initial atmospheric conditions can lead to dramatically different weather patterns over time scales of days or weeks. This sensitivity to initial conditions explain why weather forecasting becomes increasingly uncertain as the forecast horizon extends, despite sophisticated models and extensive observational data. Financial markets exhibit many characteristics of complex adaptive systems where individual agents interact according to simple rules but generate aggregate patterns that are difficult to predict. Market crashes and bubbles represent extreme events that emerge from the collective behavior of many individual traders and investors. These events often seem to come from nowhere but reflect the underlying system dynamics that build up gradually over time. Network effects create another source of complexity in social and economic systems. The value of networks often increases non-linearly with the number of participants, creating positive feedback loops that can lead to rapid growth or sudden collapse. Social media platforms, communication technologies, and online marketplaces all exhibit network effects that create winner-take-all dynamics and path-dependent outcomes. Tipping points represent critical thresholds where small changes can trigger large-scale system transformations. Climate systems may have tipping points where gradual warming triggers rapid changes in ice sheet dynamics or ocean circulation patterns. Social systems may have tipping points where gradual changes in attitudes or behaviors suddenly accelerate and become widespread social movements. Emergence describes how complex patterns and behaviors arise from the interactions of simpler components. Traffic jams emerge from the interactions of individual drivers following simple rules, even though no single driver intends to create congestion. Economic cycles emerge from the interactions of individual firms and consumers making independent decisions based on local information and incentives. Feedback loops play crucial roles in complex system dynamics. Positive feedback loops to amplify changes and can lead to exponential growth or rapid collapse. Negative feedback loops provide stability and resistance to change. Many complex systems contain both types of feedback loops operating at different time scales, creating rich dynamic behaviors that vary over time. Agent-based modeling provides a computational approach to studying complex systems by simulating the interactions of individual agents following specified rules. These models can generate emergent patterns and behaviors that help researchers understand how macro-level phenomena arise from micro-level interactions. Agent-based models have been applied to study everything from traffic flow to epidemic spread to market dynamics. The butterfly effect illustrates how small changes can have large consequences in complex systems. This concept, popularized by chaos theory, suggests that a butterfly flapping its wings in one location could theoretically trigger a tornado in another location through a complex chain of atmospheric interactions. While this specific example is metaphorical, it captures the broader principle that small perturbations can have disproportionate effects in complex systems.

Path dependence describes how historical accidents, and small early differences can determine long-term outcomes in complex systems. The QWERTY keyboard layout provides a classic example of path dependence, where an early technological choice became locked in despite potentially superior alternatives. Economic development, technological standards, and institutional arrangements often exhibit path dependence that makes change difficult even when better alternatives exist.

Self-organization describes how ordered patterns can emerge spontaneously from the interactions of system components without central control or planning. Examples include the formation of traffic patterns, the development of cities, and the evolution of language. Self-organization suggests that complex systems can develop structure and order through decentralized processes rather than top-down design. Phase transitions represent qualitative changes in system behavior that occur when control parameters cross critical values. Water changing from liquid to gas represents a physical phase transition, while financial markets shifting from stable to volatile states represent an economic phase transition. Understanding phase transitions helps identify when systems are approaching critical points where behavior may change dramatically. Scaling laws describe relationships that remain constant across different scales of observation in complex systems. Power law distributions appear in many natural and social phenomena, from city sizes to income distributions to earthquake magnitudes. These scaling relationships suggest underlying organizational principles that operate across different scales and contexts. The study of complex systems has important implications for time series analysis and forecasting. Traditional linear models may be inadequate for systems that exhibit non-linear dynamics, threshold effects, or regime changes. Understanding complex system principles can help analysts recognize when standard approaches may be inappropriate and suggest alternative modeling strategies that account for non-linear dynamics and emergent behaviors.

10

THE ETHICS AND FUTURE OF DATA-DRIVEN DISCOVERY POWER AND RESPONSIBILITY

The exponential growth in data collection, storage, and analytical capabilities has fundamentally transformed our ability to understand and influence human behavior, social systems, and natural phenomena. This transformation brings unprecedented opportunities for scientific discovery, technological innovation, and social progress, but it also raises profound ethical questions about privacy, autonomy, fairness, and the distribution of power in society. As data-driven methods become increasingly central to decision-making in healthcare, education, criminal justice, employment, and countless other domains, the ethical implications of these technologies demand careful consideration and thoughtful governance.

The power of data-driven discovery lies in its ability to reveal patterns and relationships that would be impossible to detect through traditional observation or analysis. Machine learning algorithms can process vast amounts of information to identify subtle correlations, predict future outcomes, and optimize complex systems in ways that exceed human cognitive capabilities. These capabilities offer tremendous potential benefits, from personalized medicine that tailor's treatments to individual genetic profiles to educational systems that adapt to individual learning styles and needs. However, the same capabilities that make data-driven discovery so powerful also create risks and ethical challenges. Algorithms trained in historical data may perpetuate and amplify existing biases and inequalities. Predictive models used in criminal justice may reinforce discriminatory patterns in policing and sentencing. Automated decision-making systems may make errors that have serious consequences for individuals while providing little transparency or accountability for their decisions. The concentration of data and analytical capabilities in the hands of a few large technology companies and government agencies raises additional concerns about power imbalances and democratic governance. When a small number of organizations control vast amounts of personal data and sophisticated analytical tools, they acquire unprecedented influence over individual choices and social outcomes. This concentration of power challenges traditional notions of privacy, autonomy, and democratic participation. The global nature of data flows and technological development creates additional complexities for ethical governance. Data collected in one jurisdiction may be processed and used in another with different privacy laws and ethical standards. Algorithmic systems developed in one cultural context may be deployed in others where their assumptions and biases may be inappropriate or harmful. International cooperation and coordination have become essential for addressing the ethical challenges of data-driven discovery. The rapid pace of technological development also creates challenges for ethical oversight and governance. Traditional regulatory approaches that rely on lengthy rule-making processes may be inadequate for addressing technologies that evolve quickly and in unpredictable directions. New approaches to governance may be needed that can adapt more quickly to emerging technologies while maintaining appropriate ethical standards and protections.

Privacy and Consent: Balancing Discovery with Individual Rights

The collection and use of personal data for research and commercial purposes creates fundamental tensions between the social benefits of data-driven discovery and individual rights to privacy and autonomy. Traditional concepts of privacy, which emerged in contexts where data collection was limited and localized, struggling to address the realities of digital environments where vast amounts of personal information can be collected, stored, and analyzed automatically. The concept of informed consent, which has long served as the cornerstone of ethical research involving human subjects, faces particular challenges in the context of big data and algorithmic analysis. Traditional informed consent procedures assume that researchers can clearly explain how data will be used and what risks participants might face. However, the secondary analysis of large datasets often involves uses that were not anticipated when the data were originally collected, making it difficult or impossible to obtain meaningful consent for all potential uses. The aggregation and analysis of seemingly anonymous data can also reveal sensitive personal information in unexpected ways. Location data from mobile devices can reveal patterns of movement that disclose personal relationships, health conditions, and other private information. Purchase records and web browsing patterns can reveal political affiliations, sexual orientation, and other sensitive characteristics. Even data that has been anonymized through the removal of obvious identifiers can often be re-identified through linkage with other datasets or through sophisticated analytical techniques.

The European Union's General Data Protection Regulation represents one of the most comprehensive attempts to address these challenges by establishing strong individual rights over personal data and requiring explicit consent for data processing activities. The regulation gives individuals the right to access, correct, and delete personal data, as well as the right to data portability and the right to object to automated decision-making. However, implementing these rights in practice remains challenging, particularly when data has been integrated across multiple systems or used to train machine learning models. The differential privacy offers a technical approach to balancing the benefits of data analysis with individual privacy protections. Differential privacy adds carefully calibrated noise to datasets or query results to ensure that the participation of any individual in the dataset cannot be reliably determined from the results of analysis. This approach allows researchers to conduct statistical analyses while providing mathematical guarantees about privacy protection. However, differential privacy involves trade-offs between privacy protection and analytical utility. Stronger privacy protections require more noise, which reduces the accuracy and usefulness of analytical results. The optimal balance between privacy and utility depends on the specific application and the relative importance of privacy protection versus analytical accuracy. These trade-offs may be particularly challenging for medical research, where privacy concerns must be balanced against the potential benefits of research for public health. The temporal dimension of privacy creates additional complexities. Information that seems harmless when collected may become sensitive as circumstances change or as new analytical techniques are developed. Health information collected for insurance purposes may become problematic if used by employers or law enforcement agencies. Location information collected for navigation services may reveal sensitive information about personal relationships, political activities, or religious practices that individuals never intended to disclose.

The contextual nature of privacy expectations also complicates data governance. Information that individuals are comfortable sharing in one context may be inappropriate in another. Social media posts intended for friends and family may be misused when analyzed by employers or government agencies. Health information shared with medical providers may be inappropriate for use by insurance companies or marketers. The challenge lies in developing technical and legal frameworks that respect these contextual privacy expectations while allowing beneficial uses of data. Children and vulnerable populations face particular privacy risks in data-driven systems. Young people may not fully understand the long-term implications of sharing personal information online, and their preferences and circumstances may change significantly as they mature. Educational technology systems collect vast amounts of data about student learning, behavior, and development that could have lasting impacts on educational and career opportunities. Special protections may be needed for these populations that go beyond standard consent procedures. The commodification of personal data has created economic models where individuals provide valuable information to companies in exchange for free or subsidized services. While these arrangements can benefit both parties, they also raise questions about fairness and exploitation, particularly when individuals are not fully aware of the value of their data or the potential risks of sharing it. Alternative models such as data cooperatives or personal data stores may provide individuals with more control over their information and a fairer share of the economic benefits. Privacy-preserving technologies offer technical solutions that can enable data-driven discovery while protecting individual privacy. Homomorphic encryption allows computations to be performed on encrypted data without decrypting it, enabling analysis while maintaining data confidentiality. Secure multiparty computation allows multiple parties to jointly compute functions over their inputs while keeping those inputs private. These technologies are still developing but offer promise for enabling collaborative research and analysis while maintaining strong privacy protections. The implementation of privacy protections requires ongoing monitoring and enforcement rather than one-time compliance efforts. Data use practices may drift over time as organizational priorities change or as new opportunities arise. Regular audits and assessments are needed to ensure that privacy protections remain effective and that data use remains consistent with original consent and policy commitments. Automated monitoring systems may be needed to track data flows and uses across complex technological systems.

International data transfers create additional privacy challenges as different jurisdictions have different privacy laws and enforcement mechanisms. Data collected under the strong privacy protections of one country may be transferred to another country with weaker protections, potentially undermining the original privacy commitments. International agreements and frameworks are needed to ensure consistent privacy protections across borders while enabling beneficial data sharing for research and commerce.

Algorithmic Fairness: Ensuring Equitable Outcomes in Automated Systems

The increasing use of algorithmic decision-making systems in high-stakes domains such as criminal justice, employment, healthcare, and education has raised urgent questions about fairness and discrimination. While algorithms are often perceived as objective and neutral, they can perpetuate and amplify existing biases in ways that may be less visible but more systematic than human decision-making. Understanding and addressing algorithmic bias requires both technical solutions and broader changes in how these systems are developed, deployed, and governed. Algorithmic bias can arise from multiple sources throughout the machine learning pipeline. Training data may reflect historical patterns of discrimination or may systematically underrepresent certain groups. Feature selection may inadvertently encode proxy variables for protected characteristics such as race or gender. Model optimization may prioritize overall accuracy at the expense of fairness across different groups. Deployment contexts may differ from training contexts in ways that affect different groups differently. Historical bias in training data represents one of the most pervasive sources of algorithmic unfairness. When machine learning models are trained on data that reflects past discrimination, they learn to replicate those discriminatory patterns. Hiring algorithms trained on historical hiring data may learn to favor male candidates if women were historically underrepresented in certain positions. Criminal risk assessment tools trained on arrest data may perpetuate racial disparities in policing and prosecution. Representation bias occurs when training data does not adequately represent all groups that will be affected by algorithmic decisions. Medical diagnostic algorithms trained primarily on data from male patients may perform poorly for female patients. Facial recognition systems trained primarily on light-skinned faces may have higher error rates for dark-skinned individuals. Natural language processing systems trained on text from certain demographic groups may perform poorly on language patterns from other groups. Measurement bias arises when the variables used to train algorithms are measured differently across groups or when proxy variables are used that correlate differently with the target outcome across groups. Standardized test scores may be biased measures of academic ability if different groups have different access to test preparation resources. Credit scores may be biased measures of creditworthiness if they reflect access to traditional banking services that varies across groups. The definition of fairness itself is contested and context dependent. Statistical parity requires that algorithmic decisions be made at equal rates across different groups. Equalized odds requires that accuracy rates be equal across groups. Individual fairness requires that similar individuals be treated similarly. These different fairness criteria often conflict with each other, making it impossible to satisfy all of them simultaneously. The choice of fairness criteria depends on the specific application and the values and priorities of stakeholders. Intersectionality complicates fairness assessments by recognizing that individuals may belong to multiple protected groups simultaneously and may face unique forms of discrimination that are not captured by analyzing each group separately. An algorithm may appear fair when analyzed separately for gender and race but may discriminate against women of color in ways that are not detected by single-axis analyses. Intersectional analyses require more complex approaches and larger datasets to detect and address these compound forms of bias. The trade-offs between accuracy and fairness create difficult decisions for system developers and deployers. Removing or reducing bias often comes at the cost of overall predictive accuracy, particularly when biased features are genuinely predictive of outcomes. In some cases, these trade-offs may be justified by fairness considerations, while in others the loss of accuracy may have serious consequences that outweigh fairness benefits. These decisions require careful consideration of stakeholder values and priorities.

Technical approaches to algorithmic fairness include pre-processing methods that modify training data to reduce bias, in-processing methods that incorporate fairness constraints into model training, and post-processing methods that adjust model outputs to achieve fairness criteria. Each approach has advantages and limitations, and the choice of method depends on the specific application and the type of bias being addressed. Pre-processing approaches modify training data to remove or reduce bias before model training. These methods may involve resampling to balance representation across groups, synthetic data generation to augment underrepresented groups, or transformation of features to remove discriminatory information. However, these approaches may also remove information that is legitimately relevant to the prediction task, potentially reducing model accuracy. In-processing approaches incorporate fairness constraints directly into the model training process. These methods modify the optimization objective to balance accuracy and fairness considerations simultaneously. Regularization techniques can penalize models that exhibit discriminatory patterns, while constraint-based approaches can explicitly enforce fairness criteria during training. These approaches often provide more control over the accuracy-fairness trade-off than pre-processing methods.

Post-processing approaches modify model outputs after training to achieve desired fairness properties. These methods may involve adjusting prediction thresholds differently for different groups or applying transformation functions to outputs to equalize performance across groups. Post-processing approaches are often easier to implement and can be applied to existing models, but they may not address underlying biases in model representations.

Adversarial training represents an emerging approach that uses adversarial networks to remove biased information from model representations. These methods train models to make accurate predictions while simultaneously making it difficult for adversarial networks to predict protected attributes from model representations. This approach aims to remove both explicit and implicit bias by ensuring that protected characteristics cannot be inferred from model internals.

The evaluation of algorithmic fairness requires comprehensive testing across multiple fairness criteria and stakeholder groups. Standard machine learning evaluation practices that focus primarily on overall accuracy may miss significant disparities in performance across groups. Fairness-aware evaluation requires disaggregated analysis that examines performance separately for different demographic groups and intersections of groups. Ongoing monitoring of deployed systems is essential because model performance and fairness properties may change over time as data distributions shift or as social contexts evolve. Models that are fair when initially deployed may become biased as circumstances change, requiring continuous monitoring and periodic retraining or adjustment. Automated monitoring systems can help detect emerging bias patterns and trigger appropriate responses. The governance of algorithmic fairness requires multi-stakeholder approaches that include affected communities, domain experts, policymakers, and technologists. Technical solutions alone are insufficient to address fairness concerns that are fundamentally social and political in nature. Meaningful stakeholder engagement is essential for defining appropriate fairness criteria, identifying potential harms, and developing acceptable solutions. Transparency and explainability can support fairness goals by making algorithmic decisions more understandable and contestable. When individuals can understand how decisions are made and what factors influence outcomes, they are better positioned to identify and challenge unfair treatment. However, transparency alone is not sufficient to ensure fairness, and in some cases, may even undermine fairness goals by revealing information that could be used to game the system.

The Road Ahead: Emerging Technologies and Their Implications for Discovery

The landscape of data-driven discovery continues to evolve rapidly as new technologies emerge, and existing capabilities expand. Artificial intelligence systems are becoming more sophisticated and capable, quantum computing promises to solve previously intractable computational problems, and biotechnology advances are generating new types of biological data at unprecedented scales. These developments will create new opportunities for scientific discovery and technological innovation while also raising novel ethical challenges that current governance frameworks may be inadequate to address. Large language models and generative artificial intelligence represent some of the most significant recent advances in machine learning technology. These systems can generate human-like text, images, and other content that is increasingly difficult to distinguish from human-created material. The implications for research and discovery are profound, as these systems can assist with literature reviews, hypothesis generation, experimental design, and scientific writing. However, they also raise concerns about the authenticity and reliability of generated content, the potential for misuse in creating misinformation, and the intellectual property implications of systems trained on vast amounts of existing content. The integration of large language models into scientific workflows could accelerate the pace of discovery by helping researchers process and synthesize vast amounts of literature, identify promising research directions, and generate hypotheses for empirical testing. These systems could also democratize access to sophisticated analytical capabilities by providing natural language interfaces to complex analytical tools and methods. However, the risk of errors or biases in generated content requires careful validation and verification procedures.

Federated learning represents an emerging approach to machine learning that enables training models across distributed datasets without centralizing the data. This approach could enable collaborative research across institutions and jurisdictions while maintaining data privacy and security. Medical research could benefit particularly from federated learning by enabling analyses across multiple hospitals and healthcare systems without sharing sensitive patient data. However, federated learning also creates new technical challenges related to model coordination, communication efficiency, and ensuring fairness across participating sites. Quantum computing promises to revolutionize certain types of computational problems that are intractable for classical computers. Quantum algorithms could enable new approaches to optimization, simulation, and machine learning that could unlock new forms of scientific discovery. Drug discovery, materials science, and financial modeling could all benefit from quantum computational capabilities. However, quantum computing also poses risks to current cryptographic systems that protect data privacy and security, requiring the development of quantum-resistant security measures. The Internet of Things continues to expand the scope and scale of data collection by embedding sensors and connectivity into everyday objects and environments. Smart cities collect vast amounts of data about traffic patterns, energy usage, and citizen behavior. Wearable devices continuously monitor health metrics and activity patterns. Environmental sensors track air quality, weather conditions, and ecosystem dynamics. This pervasive data collection creates new opportunities for understanding complex systems and optimizing their performance, but it also raises concerns about privacy, consent, and the potential for surveillance. Biotechnology advances are generating new types of biological data and enabling new forms of biological engineering. Single cell sequencing technologies can analyze individual cells rather than tissue samples, revealing biological processes at unprecedented resolution. CRISPR gene editing technologies enable precise modifications to genetic sequences, opening new possibilities for treating genetic diseases and enhancing biological systems. Synthetic biology approaches enable the engineering of biological systems for specific purposes, from producing pharmaceuticals to creating new materials. The convergence of biotechnology with data science and artificial intelligence creates particularly powerful but ethically complex possibilities. Personalized medicine based on individual genetic profiles could revolutionize healthcare by tailoring treatments to individual characteristics. However, genetic information also raises concerns about discrimination, privacy, and equitable access to treatments. The potential for genetic enhancement of human capabilities raises fundamental questions about human nature, social equality, and the limits of acceptable modification.

Brain-computer interfaces represent another frontier technology with profound implications for human capability and society. These systems could help paralyzed individuals control external devices, treat neurological conditions, and potentially enhance human cognitive capabilities. The data generated by brain-computer interfaces could provide unprecedented insights into brain function and consciousness. However, these technologies also raise fundamental questions about mental privacy, cognitive enhancement, and the nature of human identity. The development of artificial general intelligence, while still speculative, could represent the most transformative technological development in human history. Systems that match or exceed human intelligence across all cognitive domains could accelerate scientific discovery and technological development in ways that are difficult to imagine. However, such systems also pose existential risks if they are not properly designed and controlled. The development of artificial general intelligence requires careful attention to safety, control, and alignment with human values. Climate change and environmental degradation create urgent needs for new forms of data-driven discovery and technological innovation. Earth system models require increasingly sophisticated data integration and computational capabilities to understand and predict climate dynamics. Renewable energy systems require advanced optimization and control algorithms to manage variable generation and demand. Carbon capture and storage technologies require new materials and processes that could benefit from machine learning-assisted design.

The global nature of many emerging challenges requires international cooperation and coordination in both technological development and governance. Climate change, pandemic response, and cybersecurity all require coordinated international responses that leverage data and technology across borders. However, geopolitical tensions and competing national interests complicate international cooperation in technology development and governance. The democratization of advanced technological capabilities through cloud computing, open-source software, and educational resources is changing who can participate in data-driven discovery. Small organizations and individuals can now access computational resources and analytical tools that were previously available only to large institutions. This democratization creates opportunities for innovation and discovery from unexpected sources, but it also creates risks from the misuse of powerful technologies by bad actors. The future of data-driven discovery will be shaped not only by technological capabilities but also by the social, political, and economic contexts in which these technologies are developed and deployed. The benefits and risks of emerging technologies will be distributed unequally across different groups and regions, potentially exacerbating existing inequalities or creating new forms of disadvantage. Ensuring that the benefits of data-driven discovery are shared broadly while minimizing risks and harms requires proactive attention to equity, inclusion, and justice in technology development and deployment.

Education and workforce development represent critical challenges and opportunities in the evolving landscape of data-driven discovery. The skills required to participate effectively in data-driven fields are changing rapidly, requiring new approaches to education and training. Traditional disciplinary boundaries are becoming less relevant as data science methods are applied across fields. Lifelong learning and continuous skill development are becoming essential for remaining relevant in rapidly changing technological environments. The governance of emerging technologies requires new approaches that can adapt to rapid technological change while maintaining appropriate ethical standards and protections. Traditional regulatory approaches that rely on lengthy rule-making processes may be inadequate for technologies that evolve quickly and unpredictably. New governance models may need to combine technical standards, industry self-regulation, and adaptive regulatory frameworks that can respond quickly to emerging challenges.

The future of data-driven discovery holds tremendous promise for advancing human knowledge, solving pressing social challenges, and improving quality of life. However, realizing this promise while avoiding potential harms requires thoughtful attention to ethical considerations, inclusive participation in technology development, and governance frameworks that can balance innovation with protection of individual rights and social values. The choices made today about how to develop and deploy these technologies will shape their impacts for generations to come. The responsibility for ensuring that data-driven discovery serves humanity's best interests lies not only with technologists and policymakers but with all members of society. Public engagement and education are essential for ensuring that technology development reflects societal values and priorities. Democratic participation in technology governance requires an informed citizenry that understands both the opportunities and risks of emerging technologies. As we stand at this critical juncture in the development of data-driven discovery capabilities, the path forward requires both technological innovation and ethical reflection. The goal should not be simply to develop the most powerful technologies possible, but to develop technologies that genuinely serve human flourishing while respecting human rights and dignity. This requires ongoing dialogue between technologists, ethicists, policymakers, and the broader public to ensure that the future of data-driven discovery aligns with our highest aspirations for human society.

www.ingramcontent.com/pod-product-compliance
Lightning Source LLC
LaVergne TN
LVHW101503200926
848483LV00001B/214